Essentials for Starting
a Women's Group

Also By Pat Brill and Karen Fusco

A Topic for Everyone:
Women's Group Discussion Topics and Activities

(Currently available on Kindle, soon to be released in print)

Busy Moms: The Heart and Soul of a Home

(Currently available on Kindle and as an e-book at www.busymombook.com)

Essentials for Starting a Women's Group

Pat Brill and Karen Fusco

Table of Contents

TABLE OF CONTENTS

Acknowledgements

No book is written without support, encouragement and love from others. For both of us, our families and friends have been supportive of the time and effort we put forth in making this book a reality.

This book never would have happened if it wasn't for the wonderful women who were part of the original Women's Group started in 1997. Through their consistency, participation and commitment, the group has lasted longer than any one of us ever dreamed. Because of our experiences as members of the group, as well as our research, we learned about the mistakes that occur when starting a group, as well as what works to support the growth and longevity of a successful Women's Group.

We are grateful for the women in our group as they have become a permanent part of our lives, as well as the lives of our families and friends. Everyone who knows us knows about the Women's Group. Even the members who have moved away are still part of the spirit of the group … they never actually leave us.

We wish to thank our great editor, Jessie Andersen, for her knowledge and dedication to editing a first-class book. She not only provided the necessary eye to ensure that the work was clear and concise for the reader, she added her own perspective as both a woman and a member of her own ongoing groups. If you'd like to contact Jessie or see her other works, check out her blog at http://readbetweenthelinesbookclub.blogspot.com.

And finally, we want to thank you, our reader, to be hereafter known as the Visionary. As you start your own group, you create another link in the growing chain of women connecting. You add to the community of women worldwide who help other women become their best selves. Your journey is a wondrous one and we are there, in the background, supporting you as you continue down your path. To your success …

-- Karen & Pat

Introduction: Our Vision

From Our Small Group to the World

> Never doubt that a small group of thoughtful, committed citizens can change the world. Indeed, it is the only thing that ever has.
>
> --MARGARET MEAD, US ANTHROPOLOGIST

Pat's Story

For many years, I had a seed of an idea in the back of my mind about starting a women's group. I believed, and still believe, that women know how to nurture and add value to other people's lives. Yet we are trained to use our ability to nurture others rather than receive it from others. In a women's group, we can do both. Giving and receiving support from others changes who we are and those around us.

In February 1997, I invited a group of friends to my home with the intention of creating a group of women who help and support each other with daily living. I knew then that women are fantastic at helping others and thought, why not use this wonderful resource to create a better life for myself and others?

I asked my friends to invite their friends for the initial meeting. I brought out the easel and a large pad, and we talked about what we wanted the group to be. I had absolutely no idea how to build a strong group, but what I did have was a strong desire to bring women together. I didn't understand group dynamics and can tell you I made a bunch of mistakes, but I knew that women are stronger when they are connected with other women. Our strength is a beautiful gift we give the world.

Since we were still in the early stages of forming the group, we allowed the membership to grow to more than fifteen people. This wasn't the right number of members for us as it was too noisy and didn't provide enough time for each member to be heard. It was a great process for us because, eventually, the uncommitted drifted away and the group narrowed down to eight wonderful, committed women. Today we have five active members and four honorary members who, when they come into town, are greeted with pleasure as members of the group.

The group evolved into its current meeting structure — one that supports us as equal members of the group. Because of the equality of group members, I had to relinquish my desire to control the structure of the group and go in the direction the group wanted. Over the years, I've learned to tame my need to have the group work in a certain way and now accept and enjoy it for the value it adds to my life. It was about recognizing that what I did was important – starting the group. Now all the group members own the flow and process. Over time I've moved from the Visionary role and become an equal member of the tribe.

Ideas and dreams are important ingredients to growing a wonderful women's group. Trust your desire to start a group, for it offers so many gifts to you and others. I'm grateful I followed my idea because I am fortunate to have strong, wonderful, loving women in my life who have taught me so much, helped me through challenging times, celebrated joyful occasions with me and are a large part of who I am today.

I believed, and still believe, that women know how to nurture and add value to other people's lives. We are trained to use our ability to nurture others rather than receive it from others. In a women's group, we can do both. Giving and receiving support from others changes who we are as we influence others.

Karen's Story

I am one of the exceedingly lucky beneficiaries of Pat's initial vision.

Way back when, at the beginning of this enterprise, I was invited to Pat's house to attend a gathering of women. I had no idea what Pat had in mind, but being a close friend, I, of course, chose to attend to see what it was all about.

I remember Pat with her magic markers standing in front of her living room writing down all of the ideas we had regarding what we might want to do at this group. I enjoy bouncing thoughts off of others, and I get more creative when their thoughts are added to my own. Brainstorming was definitely fun.

Of course, I wasn't sure of all the women who attended. Many of them I did not know at all, but a few of them were familiar faces. Not friends, but I had seen them at Pat's annual Christmas open house. They seemed smart, creative and possibly people I might like.

I continued to attend Pat's meetings, and I do admit that although they were terrific while I was there, I had to make an effort to attend. Mentally, I was attending out of respect for Pat and her efforts more than for my own commitment to the group. My life was full, my work was draining, and going out in the evening was just another pressure added to the list.

What's interesting about my story is that somewhere along the way (not too far along), not only did the feeling of having to be there out of some level of obligation vanish, but it was replaced by an excitement and a longing to be with the group again, and even more often than our usual meeting time. I was hooked, and the group took on a life of its own.

I told everyone about our group – my friends, my family and even my co-workers. And to this day, I have never stopped talking about the wonderful, fulfilling bonds and sharing that have happened over the last 14 years. It is a group of women who didn't start out as my friends, but who have become some of the most wonderful people in my life.

It is and has been one of the most wonderful gifts I have ever received. Thank you, Pat, my dear and beloved friend.

The Big Picture

> *Think globally, act locally.*
>
> –PAUL MCCARTNEY

This book was created because we see the big picture. We envision what it would be like if small hubs of women all over the world come together. How would a hundred, a thousand or a million small groups of women influence the world?

We believe that when women come together for whatever reason, they make the world a better place to live. Enough small groups of women will have a significant impact on the health and well-being of the world.

As women come together and treat each other with respect, help each other find solutions to everyday living, and provide guidance and knowledge, they impact each member of the group. This influence shows up in each individual's life as they go back to their friends, family and communities and share what they've experienced with others. Eventually, it helps change the world.

This happens naturally when women come together. It's no small feat, yet it happens because of a Visionary who has a simple desire to bring women together.

We believe each group of women can help build a better world by coming together. When individuals open up to the possibility of changing their lives, connecting with others and building respect into their interactions, the world changes. Being able to encourage other women builds confidence, which, in turn, pours into all aspects of that woman's life. Her family and friends will be blessed by her deeds done with the confidence received by such an encouraging group.

What's the tipping point for this world change? It's about starting small and showing up each day to your commitment of bringing women together. The tipping point occurs when enough women follow their ideas or dreams and are willing to take the steps to make it happen. The mix between Visionary and members is powerful and as the group becomes strong and acts as a whole, the world starts to change.

> We believe that when women come together for whatever reason, they make the world a better place to live.

We want this book to travel around the world, helping women follow their dreams, and to bring together other women, one step at a time. If you feel the desire to start a women's group – just do it! You provide the vision while we provide the steps by which your vision will come alive.

Help make this world a better place by following your dream and sharing it with other women.

INTRODUCTION

Chapter 1: It's About You: The Visionary

> *Every great dream begins with a dreamer.*
> *Always remember, you have within you the strength,*
> *the patience, and the passion*
> *to reach for the stars to change the world.*
>
> –HARRIET TUBMAN

We have created this book for you, the Visionary. Since you are reading this book, we assume you have a strong desire to create a women's group. Maybe you envision women coming together to help each other. Maybe you want to build new friendships, share a common interest, or leave your footprint in the world. Whatever your reason, let's start the journey together.

What is a Visionary?

A Visionary is an individual marked by great foresight and imagination. She is a person who desires to create something – something of importance, something that has only existed in one's mind up until now. Does this sound like you?

CHAPTER 1

Can you visualize a place where women gather to share ideas? A place where they can learn from each other spread creativity, and expand their horizons? Are you missing that female connection you used to have when you were in school? Do you find yourself wanting to share thoughts, dreams and even your daily trials and tribulations with other women? Are you adventurous and wanting to be a part of something more in your life?

If so, you may be a Visionary, and it's you we're speaking to. Whatever form your vision takes, it is the seed that is about to be planted, nurtured, and grown into a beautiful flowering plant.

Taking Ownership

Taking ownership means embracing the fact that you are the driving force propelling your group forward. It means you are going to take on this job and do it well. It doesn't mean that you need to do all of the work yourself, nor do you need to be overly aggressive about it; rather, you need to keep your vision in front of you and remind the members what your vision is all about. What is important is the value of joining together and the value of being a part of this new venture.

It's funny but you will forever be seen as the leader of the group, even when other members surface up and actively participate in the growth and direction of the group. You started it. You were willing to take your idea and move it forward as a gift for yourself and others. What a wonderful way to make a difference to all who join you.

Just this small difference in their lives will impact their families and friends in very subtle, yet positive ways. These changes will spread to have an impact on the way they communicate with their neighbors and participate in their communities. And when people grow and communities change for the better, their countries and ultimately the world have been affected in a most positive way.

All because you had a vision and wanted to share it.

Can I Really Do It?

> *You have to have confidence in your ability, and then be tough enough to follow through.*
>
> –ROSALYNN CARTER

Perhaps you have anxiety that maybe you don't know enough people and won't be able to find members. Or maybe you're concerned that others will not be interested in your idea. It could be you're worried about how you will organize and structure the group, or maybe you think this isn't the right time to start a group like this. Perhaps you're apprehensive about scheduling in an ever busy world or maybe you just don't know where to start.

Whatever the reason, these thoughts can sideline you right from the beginning if your vision and desire aren't strong enough. But for those who like a bit of challenge and know they're on the right path, they will get started and continue onward.

Following through on your Vision will enrich your life and the lives of every member of the group. Keep this in mind as you journey down the path.

When we have a vision, there are no guarantees it will work out as we expected. Yet, with your desire and the road map we provide in this book, you will have a good chance to make your vision a successful reality.

Start today by recognizing you have the ability to succeed simply because you have the vision of your group in your mind. Your vision needs to be honored and nurtured. In the beginning, all you may see are things to do, problems to overcome, or overwhelming organizational issues, and you could potentially miss the most important aspect of starting the women's group.

Your women's group will truly be a labor of love, something which you have to work at and look after, something which takes time and effort, but it will be worth it. Your members will be so fulfilled and so thankful to be a part of your vision that they will constantly reward you for your effort.

If, after reading this far, you're looking for a few solid tips to help you start your group, it's time to move forward from thinking into action.

Our goal is to provide you with a thoughtful, get-down-to-basics road map so it's easier for you to move forward with your dream. What's important in the beginning is that you take ownership in moving the group forward.

So, Are You Up For the Challenge?

> *Every time we say, "Let there be!" in any form, something happens.*
>
> –STELLA TERRILL MANN

A strong desire helps you move forward a lot faster. Can you feel it? Are you willing to step out of your comfort zone to make it happen? Can you envision all the benefits for you and the other group members? Are you willing to take a chance in creating a women's group that excites you?

Are you willing to create your Vision Statement and take your first steps toward creating a women's group?

Visionary Toolkit

Knowing the ins and outs of how to develop a group and the different stages of group development is definitely important, but there's more to it than that. Your Visionary Toolkit is a set of tools designed to be used together or for a particular purpose, in this case for creating your Vision Statement and propelling your group forward.

Your toolkit includes all the questions you need to answer before beginning. It encompasses everything you should consider before moving forward and creating your group.

By the time you're done going through your Visionary Toolkit, you should be ready to put your plans into action.

Tool #1: Your Purpose – Why Do You Want To Start a Women's Group?

Step back and think about why you want to start a women's group. There are many approaches to this question.

Start by thinking about the problems you face in your daily life. Perhaps you are a mother who faces issues raising your children. Maybe you want to have greater control over your finances; or possibly you want to lose some weight, start exercising and lead a healthier lifestyle. Maybe you work from home and want to connect with other work-at-home moms.

Or, you could approach your "why" from a different angle. What are you most interested in? Is it reading, music, theatre, cooking, crafts or even shopping? Do you have a hobby or passion you'd like to share with others? What about learning something new?

Many women's groups work well with a more amorphous theme. If you are simply interested in getting out of the house to meet some like-minded souls over coffee, that might be your theme – women and coffee. Once the group gets going, you may find that you all are interested in keeping the group focused, in which case you could settle on a somewhat narrower topic, such as "women who meet over coffee to discuss their lives" or "women who meet over coffee to discuss current events."

When you understand your reasons for starting a group, you have a better chance at setting the groundwork for the type of group that will satisfy your "why."

> Your "why" is what excites you and keeps you going
>
> step-by-step through the process
>
> from beginning to end.

ACTION STEP: Create a list (short or long) of all of the reasons you want to start a women's group. You may have many different reasons that don't all go together or can't all be accomplished in one group, and that's okay. Just list them all so you can see what you truly have in mind.

This list will become the basis of your vision for the group.

Tool #2: Your Focus – What Type of Group Do You Want to Start?

Once you've identified the "why," you can think about creating a specific type of group to fulfill your needs. Rest assured there are other women out there who face the same challenges you do or share the same interests, and they would welcome the chance to exchange ideas in a group setting.

Let's say you are interested in regaining control of your finances. A personal finance group might be just the right idea – women could meet to discuss personal finance tips and tricks that have helped them in the past and financial issues they currently face. This group could even get involved with some interesting investing ideas.

This is your time to play with your vision. *Play* is the important word right now.

Use these questions to help you brainstorm your vision:

- Do you want to start a women's self-help group?
- What about reading and discussing the latest romance novels or historical fiction?
- Are you a professional woman who wants to talk to others about combining work and family life?
- Do you have a passion for a specific subject and want to study it with others?
- Would you like to go to different entertainment events together – movies, shows, ballet?
- Do you want to help others in your community by setting up a volunteer group?

The choices are endless. And this is good.

Get a cup of coffee or tea, sit down in a quiet, comfortable spot and enjoy creating your vision. Don't worry about what you need to do to get there, just allow yourself to be in creative mode and come up with ideas for your group. There will be plenty of time to think about the "to do's" that need to be done later.

ACTION STEP: Write down what type of group you want to form. Include why you want to start the group, what your group would look like, what you want to give to the group, and what the purpose of the group is.

ACTION STEP: After you have written down all your thoughts, review it and create a short paragraph that defines your group and the purpose of your group.

Tool #3: Cement and Flexibility – What Is a Must for the Group?

Since you are the initiator of the group and are willing to do the work to get the group started, it's important to know what is necessary for you and what would be nice but isn't critical.

There are a few things to consider when brainstorming your group. You need to decide how important the topic and focus of your group is. How important are things like age, stage of life, religion, background, common interests or all having children? There are also areas to consider such as the commonalities of full time vs. part time work, political views or ideals, and even the number of people you'd like for your group.

Be clear about what is important to you and flexible about what is second on your list of importance.

ACTION STEP: Write down a list of all those items that are "a must" for your group. Then write down a list of all those "nice" things that you'd like included, but are not mandatory.

Tool #4: Visualization – Get Your Imagination Going

Imagine starting a group. See everyone sitting around in a circle talking and laughing with each other. Notice their smiles. Feel the warmth in the room. How does it make you feel?

What is most powerful is your ability to imagine all the details of what a meeting with other women would look and feel like to you. How would it look to you if eight women came together once a month and bonded over a topic of your choice? Think about it. Let your vision flow.

This is the time to allow yourself the freedom to dream. What do the women look like? How old are they? Where are you– your family room, your friend's backyard, a café? How many are there – six, eight or ten? How does your meeting start? What do you do each meeting? Are you having food and drink? How are people treating each other? What are they discussing? How do they interact?

The more details you can create, the more a reality the group will be for you. As in any new project, when it actually gets underway, it's because we have first imagined doing it, experienced how we felt about it and have seen where we'd like it to go.

The list is extensive, but it's your image, and it should be fully formed. Allow it to evolve and tweak it until you feel that you have found the right image of your group.

ACTION STEP: Imagine the group as you would like to see it. Write down all of the details that you see, feel and experience when envisioning your group.

Tool #5: The Vision Statement

Your Vision Statement answers the questions, "Who are we?" and "Where do we want to go?" It is a clear, concise explanation of the focus of your women's group and what your dreams and hopes are for its future.

Your Vision Statement should inspire and energize you, and it should help you create a mental picture of your goals. It reminds you of what you're trying to build in your women's group. Even though it doesn't tell you how you're going to get there, it does set your direction and give you focus.

> Your Vision Statement should inspire and energize you!

You will not be able to create a strong group unless you are first clear about your own vision of the group. Since you are the one driving the formation of the group, this toolkit is set up to help you create clear goals and objectives. It is here that you will build a strong vision of your women's group.

<u>Create Your Vision Statement</u>

You just spent time envisioning your group and now you are ready to create your very own Vision Statement. Remember, your Vision Statement answers the questions, "Who are we?" and "Where do we want to go?" It explains the focus of your women's group and what your dreams and hopes are for its future. It should inspire and energize you and it should help you create a mental picture of your goals.

It should include a summary of what you wrote in your four ACTION STEPS.

- Why Do You Want To Start a Women's Group?
- What Type of Group Do You Want to Start?
- What Is A Must For the Group?
- Get Your Imagination Going.

This Vision Statement will be the basis of your new group at the outset, and it is what you will share with others to describe your idea of a women's group. Your vision will be crucial to the formation of your group. Without it, you would just be having some women over for coffee and gossip!

You will need to keep your Vision Statement in front of you as you get started. It will guide you throughout your journey. Keep in mind that your vision is important for you and the other members. As your group comes together, you will need to be flexible with your Vision Statement and allow others to begin tweaking it to meet the needs of the group as it develops.

> Without a vision statement, you'll just be having women over for coffee and gossip.

Each member will come with her own desires and reasons for joining, which may be similar but not exactly like yours. Allow them to add their touch to the group's vision. Every member who participates in firming up your group's Vision Statement will own it and thus, your group will become stronger.

You Are the Driving Force

You are the Visionary, the driving force that gets your group started and keeps it moving until the group takes on a life of its own. At that time, you become "just another participant" but at the beginning, there is no group without you.

What's Your Personality?

Many personality types can be successful in creating a women's group. There is no one type of personality that is best suited for the task. Both introverts and extroverts have created groups, mentored them and encouraged others to participate. It is important to understand yourself and recognize those areas of your personality where you are confident and those areas where you may need some support.

Are you very sociable? Do you love meeting and greeting new and varied people? Can you hold your own in a conversation? Does organizing a gathering allow you to shine as someone who can put it all together easily? You'll have no trouble starting a women's group provided you follow our basic guidelines. Just make sure that the group is not "all about you." Make sure that you learn how to get everyone motivated to participate and enjoy.

What if you're apprehensive about speaking in front of others? Do you feel that you don't have the right organizational skills to plan and structure a successful meeting? Are you concerned that your guests won't like your ideas or your vision? Not to worry! If you follow our guidelines you will create the comfort zone that you need to start your group and keep it going.

> Keep your Vision in front of you as you work on each step leading toward your first meeting.

A good idea for any Visionary is to find a buddy – someone who would work with you in order to decrease any anxiety you may have about starting a group. This would be someone who would share in your vision and want to contribute her efforts in the initial formation of the group. Even when we feel we can do this alone, it's more fun and reassuring to have someone as a partner.

How Much Time Do You Have?

If you are like most people these days, you already have a long "To Do" list and adding another project may seem daunting. Start by figuring out how much time you can set aside each day, week or month to organize the group. Remember that organizing is the hard part. Once you get started, less time will need to be set aside in the future.

As in all projects, we have to plan and carve out time to insure that the final deliverable is completed. Most projects are not completed in one sitting, instead they are completed bit by bit until done. It is the same for your women's group.

If you only have a small amount of time each week, create a step-by-step plan to start your group and work on it slowly. Don't worry, you'll get there – and you'll get more excited each time you sit down to work on it. If you are fortunate to have a large amount of time to devote to the formation of a women's group, then you can get prepared quickly and set an early start date for the first meeting.

As soon as you put aside the time to get started, you will find that our tools will help you move forward effectively with your desire to create a successful women's group.

Believe In Yourself

> *You can have anything you want if you will give up the belief that you can't have it.*
>
> – DR. ROBERT ANTHONY

All that is important now is that you believe it is possible to bring together a group of like-minded individuals to form your dream women's group. You don't need to know and understand exactly everything you need to do, just be willing to believe in the possibilities. You have a vision in your mind and a strong guidebook to help you. Most importantly, you believe in yourself. You have all the tools you need.

Our group was initiated by Pat. She was our Visionary. To get started, she invited a group of women to her home. All of these people had one thing in common: they were Pat's friends. Some were Pat's personal friends, some were moms of her children's friends, some were her work friends.

Most of us didn't know each other or had only met each other over coffee at Pat's house, but we shared a closeness to Pat, so we all showed up when she asked.

Motivate Others

Motivation is key to the success of a group.

As the Visionary you really can't motivate people to be interested or force them to like what they see. Instead, you will lead them by your vision and by putting in place a solid structure for your meetings and guidelines for participation in the group. On the flip side, you can easily de-motivate them by not planning well and by not being prepared for them.

You won't have all of the answers at the start, but group members will know immediately when the leader is clear about what each member could potentially gain by committing to the group. They will be intrigued and eager to find out what's to come if you lay it out properly for them.

The Strength of Collaboration

You are the Visionary with the original idea as well as the person who will collaborate with others to enhance your dream. Collaboration is an important ingredient in the success of a women's group.

When all your members contribute ideas and offer suggestions to improve your group, they share in its ownership and become more deeply committed to its success.

You have numerous resources in the other members of the group who will both support your vision and add more depth to it. Don't forget to make use of those resources.

Trust in Your Vision

> *Trust yourself. You know more that you think you do.*
>
> —BENJAMIN SPOCK

An important ingredient is to trust that your efforts will support your dream. When we work hard at something that is meant to be, we will see it come to fruition. Trust that you have the fortitude to make it happen.

Trusting in your vision is the belief that you and others will come together to create this powerful experience. Collectively, you will share in the process and in the vision. Your group will be as dedicated as you are.

Share Your Vision

In the marketing world, they say that you need to create your 30-second "elevator speech." An elevator speech is a concise, carefully planned description about your women's group that someone should be able to grasp in the time it would take to ride up in an elevator – around 30 seconds. Sometimes that's all the time we have in this hurried world.

When someone asks you what your group is about, you should have at your fingertips the important information they need to become excited to join your group. And you need to give it to them quickly and easily, before their interest wanes.

What's most important about the elevator speech is that you are clear about the focus of the group. That is why we had you create your Vision Statement as your very first step. We are more confident in sharing with others our vision when we are clear about it ourselves.

Take Action

> *Small opportunities are often the beginning of great enterprises.*
> —DEMOSTHENES (384 BC-322 BC)

Take the first steps toward this marvelous journey of bringing women together to nurture and support each other. Start small and manageable, and include action steps that will lead you toward your goal.

We've been there, we've done the legwork, and we've loved our group for many years. Now we are providing you with all the details for you to tweak according to your needs. It's all there for you to act on.

Start the Journey of Creating a Women's Group –

Be a Visionary!

V-I-S-I-O-N-A-R-Y

To take your dream from desire to reality requires stepping though several important stages and encompassing many important concepts. Our Visionary is literally made up of many important pieces.

V – Value your vision of creating a women's group

I – Initial driving force for the group

S – Share your enthusiasm

I – Ideas generated from other members

O – Open to change

N – Nurture the formation of the group

A – Acceptance and respect for all members

R – Rituals built for the group

Y – You are willing to lead

Let's Recap: *It's About You: The Visionary*

Groups make the world a better place by encouraging women to feel better about themselves and thus, spread their confidence and joy to those around them.

Now it's time for you to put your vision into action. If you've completed the previously mentioned ACTION STEPS, you've already been brainstorming and making lists, but let's make this official.

A Visionary is _____

My Visionary Toolkit: (Complete the following sentences)

      My purpose for starting a group is...

      The focus of this group I plan to start will be...

      My "must haves" for this group are...

      The things I could be flexible with in regard to this group are...

      Here's what I see when I visualize my group... (remember to include place, number of people and group dynamics)

      My Vision Statement is _____

_____

CHAPTER 1

Chapter 2: The Group is the Thing

> *To be born a girl is a gift we were given. To become a real woman of wisdom and courage is a gift we give the world.*
>
> –MARIANNE WILLIAMSON

What is a Group?

In the beginning, your group is a loose gathering of individuals who have come together to share experiences, learn and grow. You may have chosen to invite friends, strangers or a combination of both depending on the focus of your group. Deciding to start a new venture together has brought commonality among these women. Where it goes from here is limitless.

5 Stages of Group Development

All groups progress through different stages as they develop. The way they start out is most likely not the way they end up. There is growth of individuals, change of direction or focus, adjusted time schedules and more. Knowing what to expect as your group matures will be helpful for you to plan accordingly and mentor the other members in the group.

Bruce Wayne Tuckman is an American psychologist who has studied group dynamics. In 1965 he came out with "Tuckman's Stages" of group development. His model addresses the **Forming – Storming – Norming – Performing** stages. He maintains that these phases are all necessary and inevitable for the team to grow, to face up to challenges, to tackle problems, to find solutions, to plan work, and to deliver results. This model has become the basis for subsequent models.

Ten years later Bruce Tuckman added yet a fifth and final stage: **Adjourning.**

Forming

In this first stage, the group comes together and gets to know one other. It forms loosely as a group of women. This initial stage focuses on defining the scope of

> Stage one: Forming
> Getting to know each other.

the group. There is not a lot of risk-taking at this point; rather more functional discussion around the theme and mechanics of the group.

Each individual is assessing whether she can trust the other people in the room, if they seem interesting to her, whether she could fit in with others, if the subject matter is of real interest and if she has anything in common with them. In other words, can she trust that it's okay to for her to be herself without being judged?

As the Visionary, you will initially focus your energies here, helping your guests to assess the group. You want to create a clear and strong meeting structure so the members have the chance to become comfortable with each other.

Storming

This stage consists of a chaotic vying for leadership, structure, power and authority. It's where your members may have conflicting ideas on how the group should be run, what the organization should be and what the rules are. Here is where petty annoyances, competition and hostilities may surface. Some members may be uncomfortable with this interaction and remain silent while others attempt to dominate through control of the discussion or other assertive behaviors.

It's important to recognize this is a key and necessary aspect in the formation of a successful group. For you, as the Visionary, this can be a very challenging stage in your group's development.

> Stage two: Storming
> Establishing leadership and structure.

You can help the group move forward into a problem-solving mentality by fostering a process of listening. When it's your turn to talk, you should state your opinions and ideas, and when someone else has the floor, actively hear what that person is offering to the group. Impart upon your members the importance of taking turns so all members have an equal say in the construction of your group.

> *Listening is a magnetic and strange thing, a creative force.*
> *When we really listen to people there is an alternating current,*
> *and this recharges us so that we never get tired of each other.*
> *We are constantly being re-created.*
>
> –BRENDA UELAND

Another way to diminish dominance issues in your group is to form a circle that physically creates an equality of rank among your members, establishing a positive flow within the group dynamics. We will share with you in Chapter 3 the importance of a circle.

Norming

Eventually the group comes together and everyone is clear on the purpose and focus of the group. Members have discussed, dealt with and solved many of the initial problems that surfaced in bringing together different people to form this new entity, your women's group. Compromise is key to creating a functioning group. The bonds between the women in your group are formed throughout this process of working together to establish the ground rules of the group.

> ### Step Three: Norming
> Establishing the ground rules through compromise.

In this stage all members join in taking responsibility for the success of the group. This is an important time for the Visionary to start to share leadership and allow other members to be a part of the direction and soul of the group.

When you reach this stage, you have done a terrific job in moving the group through the first two challenging passages. Things have calmed down and some agreed upon organization is in place. Your members will want to contribute actively in changing or enhancing your original vision. Sometimes the Visionary has a difficult time letting go of the reins at this point, and it's important for the growth of the group to incorporate your members' ideas into your vision.

Performing

At this point the group has a strong identity and its members trust each other. You function as a unit and your members are interdependent. The group practices

> ### Stage Four: Performing
> The group practices what it set out to do, creating a participatory group full of encouragement and growth.

what it set out to do and becomes effective in creating a space where all members are participating, without encouragement, and are growing.

For example, if your vision was to start a volunteering group, at this stage all members are fully committed to the results of the group's vision. Each member sees the overall purpose of their coming together and is able to focus on the goals at hand and not on individual personalities.

Adjourning

Adjourning or ending the group comes about when your group has successfully accomplished what it set out to do and there is no need to continue the group. If your group has been one with a specific goal and that goal has been reached, this last stage may be required to dismantle the group.

It's a good idea to plan an ending ritual at this stage that would allow you to celebrate and honor the group's accomplishments and bring closure to the shared experience. Something as simple as a nice dinner or celebration accomplishes this task.

> Stage five: Adjourning
> Your goals have been accomplished and the group is no longer needed.

Not all groups adjourn. Many successful women's groups pride themselves on continuing for many seasons or many years. How wonderful when your group can continue adding new goals and new achievements over time.

Plant the Seed and Watch It Grow

Whenever you gather women together, it's a way to honor female relationships. The group's energy is powerful and developing this energy with a solid vision can build stronger lives for everyone. This group can accomplish more together than individuals can do on their own. The world has more possibilities when we join together as a group to nurture ourselves and others.

As you form your group in the beginning, you hope for strong bonding among its members. If you keep the stages of a group in mind, you will create a place where women will feel safe and are willing to return meeting after meeting.

In its early stages, you may not be aware of all the tiny seeds of interaction that are being planted to help form the group. Over time, these seeds of connection, watered with commitment and respect, blossom into strong and nurturing relationships within the group.

Not everyone is able to connect with each other at the same level, yet the whole is greater than the individual relationships. Some will get along naturally and easily with each other while others will remain more protective of themselves. Some will form relationships with each other outside the confines of the group and others will maintain relationships only within the group. As the group comes together and bonds, you travel together in spirit no matter where you go and how you get there.

Our women's group has a life of its own. For us, we each see ourselves as part of our women's group, part of the whole. And the whole is greater than the sum of its parts. We all respect the group as an entity, and we are committed to its continued growth.

It's been over 14 years, and we have journeyed through our lives together, sharing with each other, incorporating other members' perspectives into our own views, and growing stronger because we are part of the group. We have experienced the various passages of our lives with each other. When we started, some of us still had children at home, husbands, partners, ex-husbands, careers, and living parents. Along the way, children left for college and got married, husbands died, friends moved, parents passed on and yet we are still together.

Some members moved away or moved on and new people joined us. Each past member has carried the spirit of the group with her no matter where she is now. Even those who have moved away join our group meeting as honorary members when they come to visit New York. If our meeting schedule doesn't work, we always manage to make time for a group dinner out with our faraway friend.

We have supported each other through all the challenges each of us have faced. When a death or sickness occurred, each member showed up to be a part of the support system as that person faced the long journey through loss, grief or fear.

No one is ever alone in this group, and that is probably the best thing we can say about our experience.

As seasoned group members, we recognize that the simple act of coming together forms the bond. Along the way, you make adjustments, but the decision to connect is automatic.

Create the space for women to come together to focus all their energies on a topic and the outcome will be powerful. Women are strong, and when they focus their energies, anything can be accomplished.

Why Are These Groups Only for Women?

> *Groups run by women are our psychic turf; our place to discover who we are, or who we could become, as whole independent beings.*
> *Somewhere in our lives, each of us needs a free place.*
> *A little psychic territory.*
> *Do you have yours?*
>
> *—GLORIA STEINEM*

We are assuming that you are interested in starting an all female women's group and there are many reasons why this is good and healthy.

Women Relate to Women

For most women, building relationships with other women enhances their own self-esteem and confidence. They enjoy the feeling of closeness and openness shared between women who go beneath the surface. Women easily relate to other women and empathize naturally. They gather strength from being able to safely reach out to others, and by being there to support and guide someone else.

It is often the case that women become lifelong friends. How nice to be able to meet and get to know new women who may join us on our life's journey.

Women are Naturally Nurturing

For most of us, our female friends and family members nurture us, and they do it without thinking. They care for us when we are down or sick, they support us when we need it, and they are encouraging to us when we need a push.

Your women's group can provide a nurturing environment for its members too. It's an avenue where all can be supported and accepted by others, a place where you can express yourselves freely.

Women's groups support and encourage their members, give support during stressful times and celebrate the joy of positive experiences. They can create more possibilities in the lives of women and can nourish their members literally, emotionally and spiritually.

In essence, we can very simply feel grounded by the presence of a women's group in our lives.

Women Teach Women

The women we have met throughout our lives have helped shape who we are as women today. Our mothers and grandmothers were our first teachers in what it means to be a woman. Many, if not most, of our teachers in school were women,

> For women, building relationships with other women enhances their own self esteem and confidence.

successful professionals, and they provided strong examples of what it means to be a woman. We respect successful women in our society.

These women teach us by modeling. They may not even realize they are being watched. We observe how they express themselves. They mirror the qualities we see in ourselves. They help us to see our true selves by giving honest feedback. Women fill our lives with support, love, and laughter.

Our greater well-being stems from our acceptance by other women, thus allowing us to be ourselves.

Grief Support

Because women grieve differently than men, it's important to have women friends to talk to. There is a need for women to talk to other women about their grief. We need women to cry with, to express our emotions with. We need women who will rally around us when the going gets too rough to do it alone. And that is what men don't have. Where women are able to express their emotions in the open, most men aren't able to share intimacies in the same way.

No Men, Never?

There is the possibility, allowing for your group's vision, you may want to bring in men as part of building your group. We do believe that groups can

> We receive the foundation of our female selves from other women.

be effective with both male and female members, yet the dynamics that occur in a multi-gender group will create additional challenges that need to be addressed.

The first difference is that women tend to act and interact differently with men around. When men are in the mix, some women will concern themselves as to whether they appear attractive to the men – is their hair done nicely, lipstick on, etc. They may act out in trying to be noticed by the males in the group. This doesn't exist in an all-women group, thank goodness!

When some women interact with others in the group, they may be competing for a man's attention, and this gets in the way of good group dynamics. Women may not be aware of their differing behavior when men are involved, but it happens. Our reactions to this may be subtle, but they are there. Competition resides in all groups though when you include the male/female dynamic, it adds additional complexity to your group's well-being.

Our relationships with men influence us in many ways, but we receive the foundation of our female selves from other women. When we feel accepted and confident within ourselves, we offer this gift to other significant relationships in our lives. A strong women's group provides nurture and respect for all its members, and in turn, this builds the esteem of all members.

The focus of a women's group is certainly not to keep men out, but rather to come together, grow and share as women. And as women bond with other women, we ultimately have more to offer in our other relationships.

The Value Each Woman Offers to the Group

> *Act as if what you do makes a difference. It does.*
>
> –WILLIAM JAMES

When women initially come together, they focus mainly on comparing themselves to other members. They ask, "How do I see myself in relation to her? And how does she see me?" They don't readily bring their appreciation of who they are and what they can contribute to the group. We all tend to observe others when we are in a new setting, always trying to figure where we stand in relation to others.

> The strength and richness
> of a group
> lies in the belief that every
> member adds value
> to the group.

Your role as the Visionary and initial facilitator is to help them focus on their potential contributions. When you are able to do this, each member will be more committed to the growth of the group. We all want to feel we have something valuable to contribute, and we want to be comfortable enough to actually do it. In order to succeed in creating your group, you need to enhance each person's awareness of the value she offers to the group.

Your initial vision is critical to the success of the group and combined with each member's contributions, it will change and grow into something even more robust. Take some time to think about what the other members can potentially do to support your vision or help you refine it. Use all the "people" resources you have in front of you to move forward in your dream.

As the Visionary, keep in front of you the conviction that each member has something important to contribute and that the strength and richness of a group lies in the belief that every member adds value to the group.

What Are the Benefits of Forming a Group?

Not all groups focus on the same themes, so the benefits may vary within the confines of each group. We all do receive the same basic benefits when we gather with other women to form connections, even if our goals are different.

It seems to us that whenever women get busy, they relinquish their female connections. Our commitment to the group is a commitment to ourselves – to nourish and support ourselves and provide strength to others. That is a major benefit.

> Our commitment to the group is a commitment to ourselves – to nourish and support ourselves and provide strength to others.

As the group forms a solid base of commitment, each member will find it easier to:

- Create friendships that could potentially last a lifetime.
- Be surrounded by like-minded women.
- Participate in spirited and healthy discussions.
- Learn from others and broaden one's knowledge or horizons.
- Create new ideas and dreams.
- Share experiences and personal stories.
- Recharge emotions by connecting with other women.
- Reduce stress. When women get together they physically release and reduce their stress levels.

- Receive support in times of need.
- Form strong bonds with other women, which will increase one's own level of confidence and connectedness.
- Add more fun into one's life by participating in meetings, outside events and other experiences together.
- Live longer. It has been shown that when we connect with others, we extend our life expectance.
- Feel physically better due to a strong support system.
- Break bread together and connect over food.

So can you really think of a good reason NOT to join a women's group? There's so much room for growth, sharing, intimacy and new experiences that it's a shame to have it all pass you by.

What Type of Group Should I Start?

What interests you the most? What is it you want to learn? What do you have to give to other women?

Start by thinking about what you are good at, what you know a lot about, or what you have experienced. Think about what you've missed or what you'd like to have added into your life. Let it all percolate for awhile, and you'll boil it down to something that really satisfies you.

When you find an idea that makes your eyes twinkle, you've got something. If it doesn't speak to you, it may not be strong enough to sustain your group until it gets going.

The list of themes for potential groups is endless. Your theme could be very specific, such as an investing group where you study stocks and bonds, put together funds and make some smart investments. Or your group could be very general in nature, like self-help or self-growth, which would allow for an unending supply of interesting and creative topics. It's your choice and your idea.

Just to get you going, here are some ideas for fascinating women's groups:

• Personal Growth	• Medical Support
• Self Help	• Working Women
• Open Topic Discussion	• Survival as a Workaholic
• Learning Pursuits	• Theatre
• Shared Activities or Hobbies	• Entertainment
• Problem Solving	• Writers
• Professional Networking	• Book of the Month
• Political Focus	• Movie Discussion
• Single Parents or Widowed Women	• Money Management
• Parenting	• Volunteering
• Mommy & Me Play Groups	• Prayer or Spirituality
• Young Mothers	• Women's Fellowship
• Grandmothers Only	• Recipes and Cooking Club
• Mothers and Daughters	• Savings Club
• Women in Transition	• Investing Club
• Mothers of Kids with Disabilities	• Travel Buddies
• Thirty-, Forty- or Fifty- Somethings	• Honor Our Role as Women to our Families, Society, etc.

Online Groups

In this book we are assuming that all of your members are together in one room during your meetings. That may not be your vision of your group and may not be your group's reality.

There are many strong online groups where women bond. If that is your vision, you will need to adjust the structure of your meetings to add more verbal bonding in order to build strong connections with members. Maybe everyone can be on Skype together and can physically see each other even when bonding from far off places. The world is changing and there is no one way to create a women's group. The world is full of possibilities so don't be limited to your immediate surroundings.

Much of what is said here can be tailored to the online format. The basic rules for good group management and involvement still hold true. Compassionate bonding, interpersonal skills and healthy learning and sharing can occur in online groups too. See how creative you can be in this new age of computer-related conversation.

Two Powerful Currents

There are two powerful currents that occur at the same time when a bunch of individual women come together and form a women's group.

Common Theme

First, there is a common theme that has brought together all the women in your group. It is your group's focus or direction that bonds them together. It is this common theme that initiates excitement and energy in your members and helps to build the strength of the group.

The meetings are structured to support the goal or objective of the group. This agreed-upon structure enhances the ability of the group to move forward in trying to accomplish what it sets out to do.

We Change For the Better

Second, as women bond together the group's influence changes each member. Continually meeting together subtly influences each person's well-being. Women can teach each other without being teachers, support without being therapists and nurture without being family.

> *The meeting of two personalities is like the contact of two chemical substances:*
> *if there is any reaction, both are transformed.*
>
> –CARL JUNG

Ask any long-term group member what she has gained by being a member of a women's group. Each may choose different words yet the overall theme will be that each of them is no longer small, but rather is larger, more complete because of her connections with others. The world is warmer, more loving, accepting and supportive because of the connections made in the group. We have learned to be our better selves by interacting on a regular basis with other women.

Without any major awareness, it just happens, meeting after meeting goals are met, experiences are shared, laughter is voiced, and tears are shed.

Positive Growth, Woman to Woman

There are many reasons why women should consider joining a women's group. It is often said that the reason women are better than men in dealing with the real difficulties of life is because women have each other. Women have the support of their "girl" friends, and when they are thrown together in a group, they empower each other, enabling them to better deal with their problems. Men tend to want to forego that closeness with their male friends.

When women empower each other, they also empower themselves. And, for most of us, it's a lot easier talking with other women about our goals, our problems, and our vision than it is talking to men. At first it may take time to develop the atmosphere of trust that is needed before life-changing events can be discussed openly and productively. At the outset, it may seem that nothing much is going on, but the more the group meets, and the more each participant reveals about herself, the more each member is able to trust the group.

Bonding

Women face stressful situations every day. Some changes are life threatening while others are simple life changes that make it more difficult to get through the day. It may seem easiest to sit back and try to deal with these changes alone, mulling it around in your head over and over again until you think you have all the answers. But gathering together with other women is a wonderful way to improve the situation by gaining a fresh perspective and hearing creative suggestions that may never have entered your mind.

> Women can teach each other
> without being teachers,
> support without being therapists
> and nurture without being family.

By discussing our problems, difficulties or life changes with other women, we open ourselves up to a whole new way of looking at the situation. Through compromise and a steady flow of information, we can look at things differently, opening our eyes to new possibilities. And we can help other women do the same. You are empowering others while you are empowering yourself. Remember, women thrive spiritually, emotionally and physically with the help of their women friends.

> *It's the friends you can call up at four a.m. that matter.*
>
> –MARLENE DIETRICH

Although your group may initially be composed of friends and acquaintances, over time new women will join, and new friendships will be made. With some effort and luck, you will come to see your group as a second family—a family that breaks the paralyzing isolation of life-changing events by listening to the unvarnished truth with sympathy. It's important for women to bond, and what better way than to attend a women's group where your problems, your happiness and your questions don't go unnoticed?

Sisterhood

When forming or becoming a member of a women's group, the first thing you should probably ask yourself is: What do we as women have to offer other women? This can be answered with an even better question: What *don't* we as women have to offer to other women? Just think about that!

When women get together, the inevitable result is an environment of sisterhood where people can freely share their experiences, desires and woes. They can get helpful hints from other members of the group and even provide a few themselves. There's so much that can come out of meeting with a group of women even once. But it's much better when it's once a week or once a month.

Some organizations, especially churches and synagogues, offer a number of groups to their members and families. From Bible study to adult Sunday school, from informal bagel brunches to monthly dinners for couples, there are a wealth of possible activities and groups to join. However, outside the religious arena, it's difficult to find well organized support groups for women who just want to get together to grow and learn from each other. It truly seems a shame that there aren't more easy-to-find women's groups out there.

Healthy Relationships

A women's group is important for creating healthy relationships by gratifying our needs for exchanging ideas, and for gaining the emotional support needed to continue with a plan, an idea, or a life situation. After attending a group for awhile, one will soon realize that this simple getting together of women has brought with it a support system that can help you get through all kinds of difficult situations.

Many women come to see their "group" as a tool that enables them to cope with even the most difficult of situations while providing the emotional support and a wider perspective to other group members. It's a give and take situation.

Natural Networking

Networking is a great way to explore your options—not only in life situations, but also in business—and is a natural way of extending yourself and your immediate circle. Your women's group provides a relaxed forum for networking where each member may refer others to individuals or organizations they have dealt with successfully or link them with valuable connections, providing them with new opportunities.

Belonging

Every woman wants to be a part of something larger than herself and belong to something that is worthwhile or interests her. For a member to stay committed to your group, it's important for each individual to see and feel they truly belong.

Achieve Great Goals

> *Big goals get big results. No goals get no results or somebody else's results.*
>
> –MARK VICTOR HANSEN

A group can accomplish so much more than one person can. Though each person is important, they are part of a whole. If you are clear about the goals of the group and utilize each person to meet those goals, your group will perform at a high level. If your vision is a place for each member to learn and grow, then each member will need to set individual goals.

Staying Connected

In times of trouble, women want to know that their feelings, experiences, and direction are considered normal or healthy. Women have been seeking answers from other women for centuries and continue to do so today.

But things have changed these days. The hectic pace and compartmentalization of modern life makes the informal interactions of our parents' generation all too rare. Our society today is demanding enough. There often is not time for an hour or two away to attend a women's group. So we have to remember to make time for these interactions to occur.

> Women in business
> are stressed,
> stay-at-home mothers
> are stressed;
> it seems everyone today
> is stressed.

The benefit of close friendships in the group fulfills physical and psychological needs for women who may not find it any other place. With the help of an experienced group leader, information shared with members in an adult setting keeps the group on track and raises the level of fulfilling our expectations.

This interaction with other women closes a dark, unquestionable void that could otherwise continue to grow and cause physical or psychological problems. Women in business are stressed, stay-at-home mothers are stressed; it seems everyone today is stressed. Soon the stress on the body takes its toll, but you can avoid it.

For instance, by expressing ourselves to the group we can lower our heart rate, help with stress, blood pressure, the immune system and digestion. Happiness and physical health are the results of our letting go of what's bothering us. In a crisis, women offer each other the much needed support necessary to carry out a project or attain a goal.

It's not always easy for women to open up, feeling their idea or need is unwarranted and maybe even dumb. Why? Because we often don't feel our talents or skills are noteworthy or valuable enough for us to talk about. Opening up in a women's group may not be easy at first, but after networking for awhile, our doubts and fears will soon disappear.

A Second Family

A fortunate thing about a women's group is that there is always someone to spill your guts to, listen wholeheartedly, tell it like it is, and to carry you through to the next stage of your life. At some point, the group becomes your second family and telling the members your deepest darkest secrets and intimacies comes naturally.

It has been said that humor is one of the best cures for what ails you. If that's the case, a women's group can accommodate that need as well. If prayer and meditation is something that guides you, a group can lift you up and be there to listen—the key word being *listen*.

> By sharing our own experiences and listening to other members talk about theirs, we become empowered while helping others to empower themselves.

It's not about keeping things inside; it's about opening up to the group and exposing your feelings. By doing so, you are healing yourself with the help of your women friends. Your second family will be there when you need them the most without all the complexities that may exist within your primary family members. Sometimes an outside perspective is just what you need.

Acceptance and Forgiveness

Being in a women's group gives us acceptance. The more we share our experiences and personal anecdotes, the more we become bonded with the women in our group. This helps us to be able to accept and value ourselves for who we are and do the same for others.

Being in a women's group teaches us to forgive ourselves for things we have done, the things we thought would never be forgiven. By confronting our issues in the group setting, we may realize that the problem at hand lies within us, not with other people. What you may have thought was the last straw, the end of the world, or an unforgivable sin, comes to light and is dealt with in a compassionate manner. You may even discover you are not alone in your situation.

Many times it takes one woman opening up about a situation to prompt others around her to admit the same struggles. In sharing yourself, you may be helping others to deal with the same issues.

In this setting, you may notice you not only forgive yourself but are also more forgiving of others.

Personal Growth

I was always looking outside myself for strength and confidence, but it comes from within.
It is there all the time.

–ANNA FREUD

When there is a strong objective and structure to the group, each member is open to learning from others. This is when the group and its members develop new skills, knowledge, perspectives, all leading toward personal growth. As the group matures, the members will start to observe the changes and feel more grounded within the group.

Mentoring

Mentoring happens naturally in group situations. You may find yourself assisting another woman in an area of your strength, or you may find yourself seeking a woman who is more experienced than you in a particular area.

45

Mentoring is good for the soul. By helping someone who has knowledge in business, home, or relationships, you are helping to grow their ability to help themselves, as well as building your self worth. By giving the mentee the knowledge she is seeking, you are rewarding yourself by *giving back*, and what better feeling is there than that?

A Women's Group is a Powerful Thing

Positive women's groups add so much to our lives. We can heal ourselves by healing others—that's the true definition of a great women's group. We gain self esteem from group members, and we grow psychologically happier.

When a women's group has a good leader who's aware of those around her, it will thrive. The Visionary, as leader, will help the group bond initially. Over time, your leadership becomes less important and will be shared with the other members. For women who are open, loving, and caring, we can expect better health, better potential for growth, and increased happiness and well being.

We overcome crises by expressing our deepest fears, applying forgiveness, and realizing a group of women is available to help us in any way possible. By sharing experiences, working to overcome blocks in the road, and by using the power of prayer, a women's group is a powerful thing.

By allowing yourself to open up to others in the group, you can release all doubts, fears, rejections and negativity toward your abilities. By engaging in conversations, you engage in networking; and with networking, you are learning things you never thought you could learn. When all is said and done, you are giving back to yourself the worth you thought you had long ago lost.

The support system of a women's group will not only open their ears, but their hearts. That is what a women's group is all about.

Let's Recap: *The Group is the Thing*

There are five stages of group development:

- **Forming** – defines the scope of the group
- **Storming** – establishes leadership and structure
- **Norming** – discovers each group's individual 'norm' through compromise
- **Performing** – encourages growth
- **Adjourning** – ends the group.

During the Forming of the group, each member is assessing her role. She's discovering to what level she can trust the people present. Petty annoyances and competition may arise during the Storming stage, but with good problem solving skills and listening, these can be overcome.

In the Norming stage, all members add to the group's direction. The focus on goals rather than individual personalities occurs during the Performing stage, and when those goals are accomplished and there is no need for the group to continue, the Adjourning stage is completed.

ACTION STEP: In a group setting, women do many things for each other. They relate, they nurture, they teach, they encourage, they change for the better, and they receive the foundation for their female selves from other women. What is one way you could put each idea into action?

Write down your answers and then ACT!

*Note: you may not have a group formed yet. That's okay. These steps will give you practice for that time.

> **Relate:** What's one way I can purposely relate to another woman in my life?

Nurture: How can I nurture another woman I know?

Encourage: What are some encouraging words or actions I could say or do this week? And to whom?

Teach: What's one thing I feel confident enough in my own skills to show someone else?

Change: What's one thing I'd like to change about myself? What's one thing I'd like to change about my community?

Foundation: What's one thing about myself I know would benefit others? Am I generous? Do I know how to relate to others? Am I a good facilitator? Do I listen well?

Chapter 3: The Power of the Circle

> *Friends, you and me...*
> *you brought another friend... and then there were three...*
> *we started our group... our circle of friends...*
> *and like that circle...*
> *there is no beginning or end.*
>
> —ELEANOR ROOSEVELT

The Power of the Circle is nothing new—a circle represents the natural changes, flow, and graceful, constant movement in our lives.

Circles Are Everywhere

Life as we know it is a series of circles. If you stop to think about it, our lives are surrounded by circles.

Looking back into history, we can see the circle in tribal meetings and the great round tables of King Arthur. Gatherings of people from all over the world have united to form circles. Nature, in the form of plants and animals, displays circles in endless ways. From our entertainment (baseball fields) to the cycles found in nature (migrating birds) to the daily and yearly revolutions of earth itself, circles make themselves present in everyday life. Even the physical touch of a hug forms a circle. Circles unite people, placing them on equal terms.

When a circle or gathering of people is formed, each person gains an equality not seen in other shapes. Each person is the same distance apart from her neighbors. No one towers over the group as a defined leader like you might see at a gathering around a rectangular table. When we talk in a circle, our voices blend from one to the other, but not over each other. No one person has to work harder to be heard.

As you become more familiar with your group and its members, you will see how the circle plays a big role in your meetings. The spoken and unspoken words flow around the group, and as you discuss your ideas, relationships or grief, you may feel empowered by the other women around you.

What Does a Circle Symbolize?

The circle is an ancient and universal symbol of unity, wholeness, eternity, female power, the goddess and the sun. It is a never ending form, with each point leading to the next, none standing out more than the other, all equal. You will find the same in your group. All members will learn to work off one other, giving life to your circle of friends.

The History of a Circle

Stone wheels in the Northern Plains date back to 4500BC and many believe they were used for astronomical alignments. In the Native American culture it has been replaced with the Medicine Wheel, which was thought to bring people together in the circle of nature, using magnetic attraction to concentrate the natural energies in the world. It's believed to help the earth. The circle is present in everything, from the movement of the seasons, sun, and moon, to bird nests, wind, and life, everything is related to circles. But the Native American culture is not the only culture that believes in the power of a circle.

Religions of the world use circles in their symbolism and practices. The Buddhist symbol, for example, resembles an eight-spoke wagon wheel, representing the eight-fold path — symbolizing the completeness of the Dharma. In Christianity, we see circles of people used as support groups much like the one we're speaking about in this book. Christ himself had a circle of friends seen in his twelve disciples who were his support system during his ministry.

In traditional Judaism, the bride circles around the groom three or seven times as part of their wedding ceremony. The bride's circle historically symbolizes her protection of the groom and her shift in commitments from her parents to her husband. Today Jewish brides view their circles as an active moment in which she is the one who defines the familial space.

Energy Moves in Circles

Within our own circle of women, we are creating a magnetic attraction concentrating on the natural energies of human beings, which can evoke powerful healing energies for the benefit of all of us. By bringing our focus and energy to the circle, we are practicing an age-old custom, and when we leave the group, we feel inspired and connected. Enough so that when we return home, we are taking what we have discovered with us.

> *Our task must be to free ourselves by widening our circle of compassion to embrace all living creatures and the whole of nature and its beauty.*
>
> –ALBERT EINSTEIN

Within a women's group, no matter how large or small, we are given an opportunity to express our feelings without shame or fear. What we have to say stays in the group. Like ancient circle groups before us, we can express ourselves within the powerful energy flow that surrounds us. While sitting in a circle with other women, there is no one person who can claim leadership. At first the

51

Visionary will act as organizer or leader, but with time, it won't be necessary as she will become just another member of the group.

Powerful Circles in Everyday Life

> *Until he extends his circle of compassion to include all living things, man will not himself find peace.*
>
> —ALBERT SCHWEITZER

Groups of all kinds benefit from the power of the circle. When implemented correctly, businesses use *round circle* discussion to help employees. Employers have come to realize great things such as reducing company costs, raising morale, and finding efficient ways to operate are possible within a circle.

Sports teams huddle into circles to communicate moves while protecting their plans from the opposing team. Even musicians, especially large bands or orchestras, use the idea of a circle when setting up their stage. It's easier to communicate with the musicians across the circle (or semi circle in the case of musical performances) than if everyone was in a line.

As we move further into our women's circle we begin to notice there is something that connects us all. Whether the group is large or small, there are dynamics occurring within the group that define us as members of the group. Much like the Law of Attraction, which states we attract things that we need or want, we give out what it is we need to receive. And within the group, we are seeking to receive assistance, knowledge and support from other members. It's this natural give and take that binds us together.

One person may feel the group is important for unity, feeling a part of something. Another woman may feel that the group will allow her to express her feelings and concerns about her life, work, or her family without fear of being put down or made to feel uncomfortable.

Dynamics of Circle Interaction

Although groups have been recognized for years, it has only been during the last century that groups have been studied scientifically. Interest in the dynamics of groups grew in the 1980's, leading to discussion and studies of why people join groups.

Whether it's a team, a business or a circle of friends, groups give us a sense of who we are. Studies have shown that people who work within a group, in the presence of others, tended to raise their performance level. Also, to get something done requires a meeting of the minds, a networking with other members.

George Homans, in 1950, explained a group as follows:

> *We mean by a group a number of persons who communicate*
> *with one another often over a span of time,*
> *and who are few enough so that each person is able to*
> *communicate with all the others, not at second-hand,*
> *through other people, but face-to-face.*

Once we come to realize that we are not the only ones in a troubling situation, it often changes how we interact within the group. We become more comfortable and are able to share our feelings more openly. There are exceptions—not everyone is willing or able to participate in a group setting. Some women are better with a one-on-one situation, expressing their issues with a close friend or relative. Some women would rather discuss their issues with a counselor, apart from others who know them.

Your Group Circles

Group circles come in all shapes and sizes, have different defining purposes and include people from all walks of life.

Primary Groups

Everyone has a Primary Group. This is a gathering of your close friends and family. Members of this group are highly interdependent and share close personal relationships and histories, some brief and some for a lifetime. Members of your Primary Group may share activities with one another, they show concern for each other and usually provide support when needed.

Secondary Groups

Secondary Groups are made up of people who don't necessarily know each other, and interaction may be on a less personal or intimate level. They are usually established to fulfill a need or perform a function and may be short-lived rather than lifelong. They are generally organized in a somewhat more formal fashion, and one chooses to become a part of a Secondary Group.

Some examples would be a charitable group, a self-help group (such as Alcoholics Anonymous or Weight Watchers), an adult education class, and even unions and corporations.

Your women's group may start out as a Secondary Group for its members and remain that way, depending on its focus. More often than not, your women's group may transition into an additional Primary Group for its members. When acquaintances become closer friends, the nature of the group changes, and it's usually for the better.

Reflecting

When considering starting a women's group, ask yourself what your needs are and bring together those who can share with you and grow with you by being a part of your circle. Let the gathering work its magic.

So, as you can see, the Power of the Circle exists, whether it's inside a group or outside a group setting. Only we can choose what's right for each of us. It's up to us to explore what a women's group has to offer and what we have to offer other group members. Whether it's networking for employment advancement, self-help, learning something new, experiencing an adventure, exploring a shared passion, grieving, or to discuss family issues, members in your circle are there to help.

The circle is there to help you, so embrace it, empower yourself and others, give back, and mentor. It is up to you as to how much you want from this women's group. Explore your options.

Let's Recap: The Power of the Circle

Take a moment to answer the following questions:

1. What are some other examples of circles not mentioned in this chapter? Do you know of any in nature, in business, or in entertainment?

2. Where do I already see circles of people in my own life? Write down one thing about these identified circles that works well and one thing you'd change if you could. Keep these in mind when forming your own group.

3. Who are the members of my primary group? Who are the members of my secondary group?

4. What benefits do I see in bringing a circle of women together?

Chapter 4: Setting the Tone

> *Think what a better world it would be*
> *if we all, the whole world,*
> *had cookies and milk about three o'clock every afternoon*
> *and then lay down on our blankets for a nap.*
>
> –Barbara Jordan

A constructive climate is essential in a women's group. As we know, sharing and learning are essential parts of a women's group, but how can you ensure that this is done in a positive and constructive manner?

You need to facilitate effective communication, trust, honest listening while paying attention to the various learning styles that are sure to show up in your group. Adding rituals might also be of interest to you, so how do you go about doing all of these things?

Create a Comfort Zone

When starting a women's group, there are many things to take into consideration. Theme, purpose, and limitations such as age and number of members may become a concern to you. You may want to assign each member a certain role. With so many different aspects to determine and establish, one thing that often gets overlooked is ensuring that your group serves as a safe haven for its members.

It is vital when establishing a women's group to create a stress-free, comforting climate. As the Visionary and founder of this group, it is up to you to make sure a comfort zone is created so members always feel like they are in a safe, comfortable, judgment-free environment.

Build Relationships

So how you create a comfort zone for your women's group? First and foremost, you want to build relationships with each and every member of your group. Not only should you, as the founder of this group, build and maintain a good relationship with each of the members, but you also want to help foster the development of relationships between the members of your group. Closeness will ensue as relationships become stronger. This will bond your members into a cohesive unit where trust and respect are the bywords.

> It is vital when establishing
> a women's group
> to create a stress-free,
> comforting climate.

Set Ground Rules

Establishing ground rules will help to keep conflicts from arising. Our five most important ground rules, or as we call them, our "Group Success Practices" are:

- Everyone is to be treated with respect.
- All ideas are welcomed and there are no right or wrong ideas.
- One person talks at a time.
- Practice listening as well as speaking.
- Confidentiality is crucial.

Give Everyone a Chance to Speak

When engaging in discussions during your women's group meetings, make sure that everyone has a voice. It's not necessary that each member speaks on every issue in order to continue with the group, especially when some people may not have an opinion they wish to contribute. If forced to participate, that arena of safety and trust you are working so hard to build will be destroyed in an instant. We do hope that in time, everyone will learn to feel comfortable enough to say something, however short it may be.

To make sure everyone has a chance to speak out if they so choose, go around the room and give each person an opportunity to participate and have her say. For some groups, having a speaking stick, a talking object or some other prop can be useful. This is a tool where only the person holding the prop is allowed to speak until she's done. At that point she will hand it off to the next person and now it's that person's turn to speak. Of course, time limits may be warranted to prevent one person from monopolizing the discussion.

Before moving on to a new topic, check if anyone else wants to contribute any final thoughts. This way, nobody will feel left out.

Regardless of who is speaking or what they are saying, always be supportive and encourage the same from the rest of the group. Show you understand the speaker's point, even if you don't agree. This way, you can establish trust with each member, and they will realize that they will not be judged for what they say or how they feel.

Always Stay Positive

> *A strong positive mental attitude will create more miracles than any wonder drug.*
>
> –PATRICIA NEAL

It is essential that your group is a "happy place" for your members. As the Visionary, it is up to you to maintain a positive environment. Refrain from being negative in your comments and help others to follow your lead.

Whenever something negative comes up, try to find a positive aspect to discuss. See if you can move quickly from counterproductive ideas or those unrelated to the discussion at hand, to more positive, focused ideas, where appropriate.

Ensure That the Members Stay Positive

> No pessimist ever discovered the secret of the stars or sailed an uncharted land, or opened a new doorway for the human spirit.
>
> —HELEN KELLER

Don't allow negativity to permeate the group. Remind your members gently that this is a place for positive discussions and that no negativity is allowed. Members should refrain from making negative comments about each other, or even from phrasing their opinions in a negative manner.

> Don't allow negativity to permeate the group.

If you find that one member is consistently being negative, you might want to talk with her alone. Never reprimand a member in front of the group. In your private talk, you might discover that there is something going on in the member's life and you can offer your support or help. After that, remind her that the group is a place of encouragement and edification. She should share her issues with the group, so the group can move on. Alternatively, she can simply remember to stay positive in the group. A quick phone conversation might be all that's needed to get things back on track.

Never Criticize

The group is a place of support and sharing, and not of criticism. Make sure that the members are well aware of this, and that they do not react harshly to another member. Helpful feedback is far more effective than criticism.

Of course our opinions will often differ, but it is important to always come from a place of empathy, rather than a place of judgment. We can all agree to disagree, but not to put someone down for their opinions.

When topics are being discussed, members should never say "you are wrong." Instead, they should try to phrase their opinion along the lines of, "Yes, I see where you are coming from, but I feel that ..." This manner of phrasing one's opinion acknowledges the validity of another's thoughts.

> What we *think* we're sending may not be what the receiver is receiving!

By focusing on creating a comfort zone for your group, you will be providing a safe place for women to get together and bond.

Open the Lines of Communication

> *Good communication is as stimulating as black coffee and just as hard to sleep after.*
>
> –ANNE MORROW LINDBERGH

Communication is generally thought of as the exchange of thoughts, ideas, feelings, information, opinions, and knowledge. To be effective, it involves a mutual understanding between sender and receiver.

In a women's group, communication is the means by which we learn about each other, recognize our similarities and differences and share our experiences, thoughts and feelings.

To be a good communicator, one must first understand it isn't only what you say, but how you say it and how you express yourself with body language. What we think we're sending may not be exactly what the receiver is receiving! It's only over time we learn the idiosyncrasies of each person, thus helping us to interpret what and how they "send."

Verbal Communication

Verbal Communication is the spoken, oral, and unwritten way of communicating. It makes use of words and is organized into sentences. We communicate verbally with our mouths – intentionally opening our mouths to make a statement.

When we communicate verbally with others, our usual goal is to have people understand what we are trying to say. We assume they will automatically understand us. We know what we are trying to say, so obviously our message will get through. Right?

Not necessarily. Other people bring their own attitudes, opinions, emotions and experiences with them and this often affects their perception of our message. If you try to put yourself in your listeners' shoes, you may have a different perception too.

> People bring their own attitudes, opinions, emotions and experiences with them and this often affects their perception of our message.

Thinking before speaking is usually a good idea, but it doesn't always happen. Even in the heat of a healthy discussion, we may simply blurt out thoughts as they come to our minds without stopping to think how they'll be perceived by others.

We should remember positive and uplifting spoken words motivate and inspire. Thus, always try to phrase one's words positively. Negative and harsh words shut other people down and close the lines of communication. It's said for every harsh word spoken, it takes ten kind words to negate the hurt. We'd say it takes many more than that. So, one should avoid careless and hurtful language.

As the Visionary, you should recognize that words spoken affect your life as well as others. They have the power to create emotions and move people to take action. When you communicate clearly, you activate your mind and that of others. You also stimulate creativity. How you communicate will set the stage for how your members communicate with each other.

Non-Verbal Communication

Along with what we say are additional non-verbal cues into what we are thinking and feeling. Much of this comes from our body language.

Oftentimes, people do not intend to outwardly express what they are feeling with their bodies. Nevertheless, it shows. More often than not, our body language will betray a façade used to cover our true thoughts or feelings. Why? Because those thoughts and feelings are often negative or non-constructive.

> More often than not, our body language will betray a façade used to cover our true thoughts or feelings.

There are many different ways one can express oneself through non-verbal communication. It can be as simple as a rolling of the eyes or a sigh. A sigh while shifting in one's seat tends to really communicate displeasure with something or someone. Mumbling under one's breath is often a telltale sign of one's annoyance.

Posture can also speak volumes. Slumping in a chair, especially with the arms crossed, communicates that one is angry or upset. If using any of these types of non-verbal cues while participating in a women's group, your member could very likely alienate the group unintentionally.

Another emotion we tend to communicate non-verbally is boredom. Whether it is the proverbial yawn or the constant shifting in one's seat, expressing boredom through body language can make the rest of the group uncomfortable or defensive.

Another manner in which boredom may be expressed is by getting up a lot, pacing around the room, getting up for food while everyone else is sitting, or going to the bathroom in the middle of a discussion. Engaging in these types of behaviors may very well offend others in the group. This body language may communicate that the women's group is more of a chore than an essential and valuable piece of her life.

Clear Up Misunderstandings

The problem with body language is it may communicate an unintended emotion. Your member may not actually be bored or upset, but there may be another reason for her shifting or walking around. She may be a person who has a difficult time sitting still or has a small bladder. The group may misread her body language to mean something else. If this is the case, you may want to help her verbalize the reason for her actions to make sure the group understands and does not take offense at her disruptions.

Chances are that all of your members want to be at this meeting and enjoy the camaraderie of the group. As such, you should be aware that how each member carries herself will determine whether she's giving off unintended messages through her body language.

If you sense there's a general problem in this area, you might want to have a Featured Topic on "Body Language – How You Look is How You Feel." This will help them correct any negative communication they're giving out. It's sure to improve the general feelings between members.

Different Strokes for Different Folks

Each member in your woman's group will have different communication skills. When they speak, some people are clear and concise while others deviate all over the place. Some interrupt while others wait indefinitely and may never be heard. Some need lots of time to share their thoughts and feelings while others shy away from sharing anything deeper than surface thoughts.

Some members will sit still quietly while others shift nervously in their seats. Some can stay riveted on the conversation for long periods of time while others can only listen in short bursts before needing to be redirected. There's always a few who need to check their messages or answer their phones, and however discreetly they manage to do it, it is still disruptive to the group.

We all come to the women's group with our unique way of communicating, both verbally and non-verbally. As the Visionary, you should share this perception with the others and indicate the structure you have created will give each member an equal chance to communicate. It's important each member takes the time to participate actively no matter how shy or private they may be at first. It is in this way they will build a shared sense of trust and become solid members of the group.

The Essence of a Women's Group is Trust

Trust: *Firm reliance on the integrity, strength, ability, or character of a person or thing.*

A women's group is built on a strong foundation of trust. To be successful, the members must all trust each other enough to be able to open up and share their experiences freely. As we know, without sharing there will not be growth. But how can women in a diverse group learn to trust each other? How long before they can open up honestly? And how does the Visionary build that trust?

Start Small

Building trust takes time. The secret to building a trusting relationship is to start small. Begin with small, intentional acts and gestures of trust and build it up from there. It will take awhile, but there will come a time when the members of your group will not hesitate to open up to one another.

> Without sharing there will not be growth.

Think of it like dating. On a first date, you don't reveal all your deepest, darkest secrets. Rather, you check out the other person, see if he or she seems stable and sane enough. You grow comfortable with the person. Over time, as you participate in activities together, you start to trust each other more, eventually allowing both partners to open up.

The advantage of a women's group over dating is the fact that no one has a hidden agenda. Nobody is trying to break your heart or planning to leave you the next day. All the women involved are eager to share their lives and support of each other – it just takes a few steps to build a strong relationship among the members of the group.

You can help to build the members' trust in each other by starting off with small non-invasive exchanges. At the first meeting, everyone will want to share a few broad details of their lives – what they do, what their family status is, and what they hope to achieve within or get from the group. That's enough delving to start with.

It's important for the Visionary to begin this process. She sets the standard of trust. If she is willing to share, the others will be more willing to share.

Build Gradually

> *It takes a lot of courage
> to show your dreams to someone else.*
>
> —ERMA BOMBECK

Build up the relationships from there. At each meeting, have all members contribute something more about themselves, sometimes large and sometimes small.

For instance, in a parenting group, one member might bring up that her son has tantrums and mention how much trouble she has in stopping them. After hearing her problem, other members might join in, confide that they had the same issues when their children were younger and offer some suggestions. When one person opens up, others feel free to open up as well. It's less scary when someone else goes first.

Members may feel uncomfortable opening up because they're scared of being ridiculed or hurt. Some people can be very judgmental and may speak without thinking. Of course, in a women's group people are more supportive, but it takes time to prove that support. As one woman opens up, others will start sharing their thoughts and experiences as well.

Trust is a matter of give and take and does not happen in an instant. You can't force the group members to trust each other; it won't work. It has to come naturally.

Try a Gratitude Round

You can try some sharing activities to speed up the process. One such activity is a "gratitude round" where each woman is asked to list the three things she is most thankful for since the last meeting. They can be deep or they can be light. This helps the members to share their joys and their hopes. When everyone exchanges their news at the beginning of each meeting, members will start to know more about each other. This increased knowledge means members will become closer, each letting the other members in a little bit at a time – again, breaking down barriers and leading to increased trust.

The important thing to keep in mind here is trust does not happen overnight. Each member's integrity, ability and character will become more visible as time goes on. As long as members are participating together in a positive, constructive manner, trust is sure to follow naturally.

Give the relationship among the members time to develop, don't rush things and watch how your group matures and grows closer.

We have one member who is private and reluctant to share feelings and issues with the other members. Several years passed before she started to disclose issues that had occurred in her life. It took her a bit more time to speak about issues as they were occurring. Today, she still is private but feels safe enough within the group, with a little bit of coaching, to share more about herself. All members respected her need to slowly build trust with the group members.

Sense Your Learning Styles

That is what learning is. You suddenly understand something you've understood all your life, but in a new way.

—DORIS LESSING

When you start a women's group, it's important to keep in mind that different people learn in different ways. Remember when you were in school and you learned best by listening to someone explain the concepts, while your friend learned best by taking notes? That's an example of differing learning styles in action. The same holds true for participating in a women's group – different women learn in different ways.

There are three commonly recognized learning styles.

Visual

Visual learners learn through seeing. They think best in pictures. As an example, in a cooking group, the visual learners will learn best by watching videos of the recipe actually being made.

> Visual learners learn through seeing.

Auditory

Auditory learners learn through listening. Discussions work best for them. In our cooking group, the auditory learners will learn best by hearing someone explain the different steps in the recipe.

> Auditory learners learn through listening.

Kinesthetic

Tactile/kinesthetic learners learn through moving, doing, and touching. They learn best by actually implementing the steps themselves—a hands-on approach.

> Tactile/kinesthetic learners learn through moving, doing and touching.

Following through with our cooking group, they will "get it" when they actually mix the ingredients together and put the mixture in the oven.

CHAPTER 4

Multiple Intelligences

The Theory of Multiple Intelligences, proposed by Howard Gardner in 1983, also helps us to analyze the wide variety of cognitive abilities. These go hand in hand with the learning styles just mentioned. One such intelligence is Linguistic. These learners learn best through words and enjoy gathering information by using reading materials. In our cooking example, this learner could easily create a dish with a recipe in front of her. A group focus on a book would be of particular interest to this person.

There are also Interpersonal and Intrapersonal intelligences. The interpersonal person is an extrovert and likes to work in groups. She learns best by bouncing ideas off others. The intrapersonal person, on the other hand, is introspective and prefers to mull things over in her own mind. She likes working alone and may find it more difficult in a group setting.

Variety is the Spice of Life

It is important to keep the different learning styles in mind when you plan how to structure your meetings. Your group most likely will consist of different types of learners. One interesting women's group activity is to take a "learning style test" together. This is a fun quiz that allows members to understand their style of learning and what it means, whether they are visual, auditory or kinesthetic. You might try this easy quiz at:

http://people.usd.edu/~bwjames/tut/learning-style/stylest.html

A side benefit of this quiz is you will also find out how many visual, auditory and kinesthetic learners you have. With this knowledge, you can optimize your meetings and activities to focus on the learning styles in your group.

For members who learn visually, it is important to describe the look of things. A few pictures, photos or videos are especially helpful. Since they learn visually, they might also be quite good in design or possess artistic skills. They may be happy to contribute by taking photographs or designing the group website.

70

Your auditory learners will enjoy listening to speakers on tape and then discussing with the group, closing their eyes and learning about progressive relaxation, or enjoying studying different musical styles. They will be able to reflect well upon all that has been said at one of your meetings, and thus, may be very engaged during your Featured Topic presentations.

> Due to different learning styles, we will all contribute differently.

Kinesthetic learners will enjoy participating in group activities, they are do-ers. They may like to create something physical or problem solve as a group. They probably will prefer group activities that require moving around the room rather than sitting still. Keep in mind that kinesthetic learners may seem slow to understand something initially, but that is generally because they need to put things in practice before they really understand it.

Because we all have different learning styles and multiple types of intelligence, we will all contribute differently as well.

A kinesthetic learner will describe how something is done, while an auditory learner will talk and listen to the other members. A visual member will enjoy contributing her artistic design skills to the group.

To say it simply when it comes to learning, variety is the spice of life.

Listening – An Essential Skill

Listening is an absolutely essential life skill and it's a very important tool in your women's group. You will want to promote good listening skills for all your members.

Build Rapport

Listening is a way of building rapport; it strengthens the bond between the talker and the listener. When you listen to someone, you learn more about them. You understand what's going on in their life, how they think, where they're coming from, and what experiences they are drawing from. In turn, the person you are listening to feels you understand them better; they are thankful for the support and the empathy you provide them by being a good listener.

Practice Good Listening

> There are people who,
> instead of listening to what is being said to them,
> are already listening to what they are going to say themselves.
>
> —ALBERT GUINON

Practicing proper listening skills will help you build strong connections with the other members and will help you get the most out of your group experience. Good listening skills are more than just sitting listlessly while somebody else talks. In a group, there's a big difference between active and passive listening.

First, you have to really want to listen. Don't just hope she'll stop talking soon – try to actually understand her! Be an *active listener* and attempt to understand what she's saying. Put yourself in her shoes and empathize with what she is sharing. The instant you do this, you will find you are a much better listener, and this will inevitably bring you closer to the talker.

As a good listener, you will want to show off the fact that you're listening. This means nodding as someone else talks, looking them in the eye and making the right verbal cues, like saying "uh-huh", "exactly" and "mm-hmm." We as women do this pretty much automatically. Unfortunately, because we tend to do this automatically, we need to be careful that we really are paying attention to what's being said, responding with appropriate comments that are relevant to what the person is sharing.

Respond Appropriately

Showing proper reactions while someone is talking is also important. If they say something funny, laugh. If they say something surprising, raise your eyebrows and look surprised. Again, we women do this naturally, but it's important to keep in mind that listening is the response to talking – so you shouldn't hesitate to show your response.

Of course, if your reaction differs from the naturally expected one, don't feel obliged to just go along with what's being said. Make sure, however, the talker has truly finished telling her story before you offer an opinion.

Let's say someone is telling you their woeful mother-in-law tale. Don't hesitate to tactfully sympathize with the in-law – you might be able to actually help the relationship by expressing the in-law's potential perspective. Differing in your opinion is also a part of listening – it shows you've paid attention and can offer another viewpoint on what's been said.

Being a good listener also means never interrupting someone, or being over eager to express your views. Most of the time, we just need a "still spirit" to hear our stories. Fortunately, when you participate in a women's group, you will have plenty of opportunities to be both the listener and the talker.

Stimulate Creative and Critical Thinking

If you are the facilitator of a women's group, you will come across multiple instances requiring creative and critical thinking. Such instances could include discussing a problem posed by a group member, discussing and analyzing a book or movie, or coordinating a volunteer effort.

Regardless of the reason, there are a few helpful techniques used to stimulate creative thinking.

Brainstorming

> *If everyone is thinking alike, then somebody isn't thinking.*
>
> —GEORGE S. PATTON

To get started, one person must be designated to take notes. Members can volunteer for this position, or they may be assigned the note-taker position on a revolving basis. It helps to have a stand up easel or pad and colorful magic markers so the note-taker can write everything down for all to see.

Create a playful environment to stimulate creative ideas. Even if the topic at hand is something very serious, refrain from getting bogged down or from trying to be somber. Playfulness stimulates creativity, so create a light-hearted environment – having comfortable seating and snacks on hand can make this much easier.

Identify the topic you need to brainstorm. Perhaps you're discussing overcoming debt, managing an unruly teenager, or planning a group vacation.

> Brainstorming is a method of generating many ideas while placing judgment on hold.

If your group has never done this before, warm up by practicing brainstorming on a funny and rather ridiculous topic – this will also help to heighten the playful mood. For instance, you might want to come up with a new game for the Olympics or a new breed of cat. After the warm up session is over, everybody understands how it's going to work and you are ready to move on to the main topic at hand.

There are a few ways in which brainstorming can be done. People can take turns in suggesting a solution out loud, or they might have one minute each to list their suggestions on paper. The group might start off with three silent minutes to think about the issue before offering their thoughts, after which they can piggyback off each other's suggestions.

When brainstorming, it is important to suspend judgment and focus on coming up with as many ideas as possible. Make sure everyone in the group knows that ALL ideas are good and valuable. Afterwards, you can go through the ideas and whittle them down to the ones you (as a group) would like to focus on.

What If?

Another way of stimulating creativity is to play the "what if" game – what if XYZ were true? If the "what if" is 'What if rocks were soft?', then the answers might be "We could use them as pillows" or "We could grind them up to use as carpeting." Of course, they wouldn't be of much use in concrete... and so forth.

Mixing Senses

Another way to stimulate creativity is to exclusively think of things in terms of colors or smells, and to alternate the senses that are normally associated with things. What does a wall smell like? What color is perfume? What does a happy thought taste like? How does a beautiful melody look?

There are a number of other tactics for stimulating the creativity of a group, but these should give you a start. The important thing to remember in all these exercises is everyone should get a chance to participate, and nobody should be judgmental about the others' responses.

Rituals Solidify a Group

A great way of forging bonds within a women's group is to create group rituals. These rituals are reminiscent of the "secret society" rituals we all participated in as young girls. They make group members feel like part of something special.

When we all participate in a group ritual, we feel a greater connection with the other participants, especially if the ritual is something meaningful for us. It's something unique to our group, and only we experience it together.

Ambience Rituals

It's easiest to do if the meeting is being hosted in someone's home. For a sense of serenity, you can set the mood with soft lighting, candles and incense or oils. Background music may add a nice touch.

> Creating the right ambience
> for your meeting
> sets the tone.

Check to see if any member is allergic to incense or candles. If they aren't, you might want to select a "group scent" by lighting a specific scented candle for each meeting. In fact, you may even wish to buy one of the large scented candles and light that same one at each meeting. If the meeting is held in rotating homes, each host can keep the candle at their house and pass it to the next host as part of the closing rituals.

Circle Around

We have spoken about The Power of the Circle. Now it's your chance to carry that through to your women's group. Select a physical space that will allow you to create a circle of just the right size to include everyone attending. Not too big – we want our group to be focused and intimate. And not too small – leave enough room for comfort as you're going to be there for awhile. No crowding in five people on one couch!

Opening Rituals

An opening ritual is a great way to start the formal portion of your meeting. As each member arrives, they will probably exchange pleasantries. Ask everyone to wait until all are present before exchanging news. Once everyone has settled in, give everyone a chance to update the others on their personal news.

After all have had a chance to say hello and speak briefly, you might want to conduct a short group meditation or prayer. This is a wonderful way for everyone to quiet their minds before focusing on the topic of the meeting. Meditating together in a group will also strengthen the members' bonds with each other.

The Talking Object

It is essential to take turns in a group. Many times one member will be talking and others may interrupt without warning. This can be disruptive to both the person who was speaking and to the group in general. So we recommend creating a symbol that indicates whose turn it is to speak.

> We recommend creating a symbol that indicates whose turn it is to speak.

Your "talking object" might be a decorated stick, a cushion, a painted stone, a large seashell, or a statuette. You might choose something related to the focus of your group like a paperweight in the shape of a pot for a cooking club, a badge in the shape of a book for a book club, etc. You get the point.

There are two important aspects to the talking object. First, whoever holds it is the one who is empowered to speak. And secondly, whoever is not holding it is empowered to listen. Both roles are important as we want to both actively talk and actively listen.

Choose a meaningful symbol that members will pass to each other to indicate who has the floor. And make sure everyone adheres to this rule so each person can have her turn to speak freely.

Closing Rituals

Don't neglect the closing rituals. They not only bring closure to your meeting, but allow you to set up for what's coming up next.

Your closing ritual may include a final meditation, a symbolic blowing out of the group candle, or a relaxing stretch. It can also be very informal with everyone simply acknowledging each other and making sure to say goodbye to each and every group member.

Some groups keep a notebook recording "minutes," but it doesn't have to be that formal. Simply enter some wrap up comments, jot down a few bullet points and record the activities of the meeting. Members can take turns doing this so everyone gets a chance to participate.

Make a date for the next meeting, settle on a location and be sure to remind members to make a note of it. Yes, write it down right then and there!

Thank everyone for a great meeting and pass the candle or incense to the next host. Always make sure to end the meeting on a high note – say things in a positive manner to ensure everyone retains a happy memory of the meeting.

Some Topics May Be Taboo

Certain topics can create an awkwardness between members and may be divisive, especially when the group is very new and people are uncertain of others' leanings. It may be beneficial to ban some controversial topics from your group's discussion.

Unless you're a politically motivated group, it may be a good idea to keep politics out of any discussion. Politics tend to bring a lot of different opinions with a lot of passion behind them. As such, making politics a taboo subject is often the wisest choice.

> Making politics a taboo subject is often the wisest choice.

Unless you're a Bible study group, religion is also a subject that potentially should be considered taboo. Otherwise, there is a good chance arguments will invade the group. Such situations could quickly make the group an uncomfortable place for many of the members, ultimately resulting in the disbanding of your group.

Though it might seem a bit harsh to make certain topics off-limits, you will find that such topics can really polarize a group and create ill-feeling among members.

There are certainly other issues that are bound to lead into heated conversations, and those should be limited or taboo altogether. Not every subject is right for every group of women. What part of the world you live in and what is considered polite conversation will help determine what your group wants to concentrate on and what should be left to another day.

When our women's group got together, it was supposed to be all about us as women. It was very easy for us to be moms and start talking about our children and their issues, but that was not what we were there for. We were supposed to be improving ourselves, growing and learning – it was supposed to be strictly for us.

So we very quickly banned all conversation about our children. It wasn't easy, but it allowed us to focus more clearly on ourselves.

Let's Recap: Setting the Tone

- Create a comfort zone
  - ➢ Set the ground rules
  - ➢ Stay positive
- Open communication
  - ➢ Be aware of non-verbal communication
- Trust
  - ➢ There is no growth without trust
  - ➢ Start small and grow from there
  - ➢ Use a gratitude round or other trust building activity
- Learning styles
  - ➢ Visual
  - ➢ Auditory
  - ➢ Kinesthetic
- Listening
  - ➢ Be an active listener!
- Creative Thinking
  - ➢ Brainstorm – no judgment allowed
  - ➢ What If?
  - ➢ Mixing Senses
- Rituals
  - ➢ Talking object
  - ➢ Opening and closing rituals

Chapter 5: How Do I Get Started?

> Congratulations! Today is your day.
> You're off to Great Places!
> You're off and away!
>
> —THEODOR GEISEL

Group Basics

Congratulations! You've decided to start a women's group, and now there are lots of things to think about and lots of planning to do. It may look overwhelming to you right now, but no worries, we'll break it all down so you can get started and be successful. So let's think first about the first things to do.

What Is the Focus of Your Group?

You've already thought about what kind of women's group to start. Maybe you haven't crystallized what it will be or what your goals are, but you have some ideas. Will it be simply a group that gets together to discuss open-ended women-related topics? Will it

> Whatever your choice
> of focus is,
> it's just a starting place.

focus on interpersonal relationships? Will it be all about self-help and personal growth for women?

Do you have a particular activity or hobby you want to share with others? Maybe reading and discussing the latest best-sellers, teaching each other new dishes to cook, going to and discussing plays or movies. What about learning all about investing or improving ones financial health?

Whatever your choice is, it's just a starting place. You will present it to your prospective members and those that sparkle at the thought will join you on your journey.

What Type of Group Will This Be?

There are some groups that enjoy sharing each meeting with the same people every time, and only those people. Other groups prefer to invite members from a wider audience, never quite knowing exactly who or how many will show up. The subject matter and location you choose have some bearing on this.

If your group is a study group of some kind, you may have rotating members who stay for a period of time and then move on depending on the topic of study. New members may join at any time.

If your group is more structured and the women become friends, your group will be better suited to being a set selection of women who attend every meeting with outsiders only attending with the thought of becoming permanent members.

If you're meeting in someone's home, certainly they'd like to know ahead of time how many to expect. If your meeting is in a public space that can accommodate a larger group of women, the more the merrier!

Closed Groups

A closed group is one where the group has a set number of members who have committed to attending every meeting and are interested in sharing the vision and voyage of growth together. Your group should have in mind a maximum number of women, and when that number is reached, the group is closed.

New members are not entertained on a regular basis unless someone leaves the group. Potential new members can be invited to come to a meeting to see both if they'd like to join and if the group feels it would be a good fit.

> Closed groups have a set number of members who are committed to the growth of the group and its individuals.

Open Groups

An open group is one where there is a larger pool of women who are part of the group, and the expectation is that not everyone will attend every meeting. There may be twenty people who have expressed an interest in participating on a semi-regular basis and this is your pool to draw from. There is still a "closed" element to this group in that new people not already in the pool are not invited without first discussing it with the group members.

Your group should have in mind a proposed maximum number of people acceptable for any one meeting, and when that number is reached, the group turns from an open group to a closed one. This may be different depending on the location. Some people can only accommodate a certain number of people in their home, which is why it's important to sign up if you plan on attending that meeting.

> Open groups pull from a large pool of women who may not all attend every meeting.

Over time you will find that there will be a core group of women who tend to come to every meeting and others who attend less frequently. At some point the group may morph into a closed group or it may continue to enjoy having a variety of members showing up and contributing in different ways, leading to varied interactions between the members.

One open group Pat has participated in is a themed group, specifically a Spirituality Brunch, and there are about twelve people who have attended at least once. These women are regularly invited, with the expectation that only about eight will actually show up to any one meeting. Everyone brings a dish to contribute to the brunch and the topic is always related in some way to spirituality. Even though not everyone is at each meeting, this group works because its attendees have all gotten to know one another, and everyone is aware that there will be a different mix each time.

Drop-In Groups

A drop-in group is one in which new attendees are welcomed at every meeting. They can simply "drop in" because they are aware of a specific topic that interests them, or they have chosen to come along on an outing. There will be a core group of women who tend to come to every meeting, but new attendees will change the flavor of each get-together.

> Drop-in-groups have a core group of women as well as new attendees who are welcomed at each meeting.

Here too, you should have in mind a maximum number of people acceptable for any one meeting, and when that number is reached, the group is closed until the next meeting. So it is important for people to sign up or get in touch with the Visionary ahead of time to let her get an accurate head count.

Meetups (www.meetups.com) is a great example of Drop-In Groups. Their goal is to help groups of people with shared interests plan meetings and form clubs in local communities.

The focus of this book is concentrated mainly on closed and open groups. But many of the ideas and suggestions will work for the Visionary who wants to begin a drop-in group too.

Rules of the Road

Before you can expect the group to adhere to any structure, you yourself must be clear about the essential ingredients needed to cook up a quality group.

Listening Without an Agenda

Everyone who participates in your group will want to be heard. It is up to you, the Visionary, to make sure your members are also good listeners. Being a good listener requires one to not only hear the speaker, but actually pay attention to what is being said. That's called "active listening."

And when you listen, remember all ideas are welcomed equally. You are not there to convince someone of your own agenda or to sway to your side of an issue. You may agree or disagree with what the speaker is saying, but it is not for you to comment on where someone else is coming from. This is not a time to give advice, just a time to hear what others say and think. Your women's group should be an open forum for ideas without fear of criticism or rejection.

Shared Ownership

You as the Visionary will be the initial leader of the group. You have the idea, the will to get started, and you guide the direction of the group. You are bringing diverse people together and setting the stage for a women's group that will take on a life of its own.

As your group evolves, it will be expected that other members take over various roles in managing the group. When that happens, the ownership of the group will no longer be solely yours. As soon as you see a strong person stepping up and taking a leadership role, relinquish a bit of your role as the Visionary.

> It's ideal if everyone participates,
> takes on a role and supports
> the overall objective
> of the group.

85

Ultimately, it would be ideal if everyone participates, takes on a role and supports the overall objective of the group. We have found it a very good idea for each person in the group to be counted on for some responsibility, however small it might be. That gives each person a tangible stake in the continued success of the group.

Confidentiality

We cannot stress enough how important it is to establish confidentiality or intimacy in your women's group. Certainly topics of interest may be discussed freely with one's friends and family, but it must be clear that any and all private information or feelings is to be a part of the group ONLY and not be shared with others.

Some members may share very sensitive or revealing information within the confines of the group experience and will have the expectation that their secret is safe. Confidentiality is crucial, and it is the main ingredient that will lead to the members being able to trust each other and trust the solidity of the group.

<u>Sharing Secrets is a No-No</u>

It is absolutely essential to keep the group's discussions private. Whatever is said during a group meeting is to be shared only with the group members. This means no sharing of even the trivial things. What might seem trivial to you might be a larger issue to someone else. For instance, a member might share the fact that her son is having troubles with bed wetting. This might not seem like a big deal to you, so you mention it to your husband. If your own child overhears this, he might tell others at school, unintentionally heightening the taunts and teasing. This has the potential to further worsen the problem for the bed-wetter – an unintended, but unpleasant outcome.

Sharing a secret means just that – sharing it with the world. It will no longer stay a secret and will eventually reach the ears of a lot of people. It would be quite disastrous if it got back to the initial member who shared her secret; but even if it doesn't, it reflects badly on you and your group.

Remember, your group is separate from the rest of your life, and no matter how much you trust someone outside the group, keep in mind that the group members do not know and trust that person. She is not their friend or confidant and may not choose to reveal such information to him or her.

Protect the Sanctity of the Group

You should always be protective of the sanctity of the group and remember that the group is a refuge for you and the other women. Down the road, the group will be a pillar of support. If one member violates the trust existing within the group, the group may exclude her slowly, or may ban her from the group entirely, and all the hard work of participating and creating bonds will go to waste.

Therapeutic, Not Therapy

The group is not meant to be therapy, rather it has therapeutic value. People will learn and grow emotionally and intellectually by participating in your group, but this is not a place to come to for personal advice. For purposes of the group, we do not purport to be professionals in that area, even if we are therapists in our own right.

Commitment

Some members of your women's group will show up faithfully to all meetings, ready for a great experience. Others will have "more important" things to do, which get in the way of participating in the group fully. One week there'll be a dinner scheduled with a friend, another week it will be a date with a new guy, and yet another excuse will be a vacation.

> It's that person who only shows up intermittently that really takes a toll on the other group members.

Of course everyone will have something unexpected arising that gets in the way of showing up for a regularly scheduled meeting, and that's okay; but absences should be the infrequent exception rather than the rule. It's that person who only shows up intermittently that really takes a toll on the other group members.

Making a Commitment to Commit

Your members should make a promise to themselves and to the group to be there, both physically and mentally, whenever and wherever the group is meeting. Being a member of a women's group which meets regularly means you need to make the time commitment to show up for each meeting and to be mentally present. It's called being engaged in the group.

Those who truly commit to the group gain for themselves and help solidify the group entity.

Special Friendships

Regular attendees form special friendships and bonds with one another. An occasional attendee will miss out on this camaraderie.

Connections and Trust

Regular attendees may feel resentful toward an occasional attendee for not considering them and the group important enough to make a commitment to be there more often than not. This will certainly set that person apart from the rest of the group, and not in a good way. Connections with others deepen and trust is fostered when everyone participates at the same level.

Consistency

Failing to make it to the meetings on a regular basis will also cause a member to miss out on valuable information and experiences that take place during the meetings. The more she misses, the more of an outsider she will become. Later meetings will likely involve some fun chit-chat about something that happened at an earlier meeting, and she'll feel left out because she wasn't there for those happenings. As a result, she won't be able to participate in the conversations taking place. She'll likely also miss out on many an inside joke that came out of those missed meetings.

> So we like to state our general level of commitment as follows:
>
> ### Nothing is more important that the group.
>
> And from there, we make our exceptions.

Be On Time

Part of being committed to a women's group is to make a solid attempt to arrive on time. Every so often one might get caught in traffic or have an unexpected delay, but it's very disruptive if people show up late consistently. And it shows a lack of respect to the other group members. Remind your women's group that timely arrivals allow for timely endings.

What Roles Are Needed?

Every group has certain roles needed to be fulfilled by various members. Not everyone will need to take on a role, but it's best to share these responsibilities so no one person has to do everything. Encouraging participation of your members by asking them to rise to the occasion and taking on a piece of managing the group helps keep everyone interested in the group's wellbeing.

There are two categories of roles that arise in most groups. Some roles are filled by a different member each meeting and others are held by one individual for an extended period of time.

Rotating (or Revolving) Roles

Rotating roles are those which are filled by a different member at each meeting. This allows for shared responsibility and prevents one person from always being in the same position. This is especially important if that role may be uncomfortable or may ask too much from one person.

Hostess

Each meeting will be hosted by one person in the group. If the meetings are held at members' homes, the Hostess is the one whose home is being used. If the meeting is at a public place, there is still a need for a Hostess and it should rotate. This Hostess is responsible for making sure the room is set up to accommodate all members, any refreshments are provided for and your "guests" comfort is attended to.

Facilitator – Topic Presenter

At each meeting there will be a topic or activity that serves as the main part of your meeting. One member will be the Facilitator, and she will be responsible for deciding upon a topic and presenting it to the group. She will also be responsible for bringing any necessary supplies needed to complete this activity, such as paper and pencils, visual aids, or preprinted writings.

This is a very big job and will change at each meeting. You will find that some members are more comfortable coming up with topics while others will have more trouble, but everyone should be encouraged to take a stab at it.

> *In our group, the Hostess and the Topic Presenter have always been one and the same, and this is fine to do. The woman whose house is being used for the meeting has had to generate the topic, provide supplies and keep the meeting on track. We have gotten used to it this way and it works well for us.*

We recognize it may be more difficult in your group having the Hostess also be responsible for the topic presentation. After all, it's a lot of pressure to serve the food, make your guests comfortable, organize the topic and keep everyone on track. It's hard to be running in and out of the kitchen and staying focused on the discussion. We suggest thinking about keeping these roles separate.

Timekeeper

At each meeting, one person should be in charge of monitoring the length of time each member is allowed to speak. If your group decides a turn is to be three minutes, then the Timekeeper's job is to move the conversation along when a member is speaking more than three minutes. She should gently suggest to the person that she should wrap up; and if that doesn't work, she must be a bit more forceful, always remembering to be tactful.

As long as everyone in the group understands the purpose of the Timekeeper, no one's feelings should be hurt when asked to move on. As you can see, this is one job that should rotate between members so no one person has to become that bad guy that everyone glares at.

The Timekeeper may also help keep everyone focused on the topic. If people's attention wanders and they start chatting in small groups, the Timekeeper should ask everyone to tune in and be respectful of the woman who has the floor. In addition, the Timekeeper should tactfully remind any interrupters that the person with the talking object is the only one who should be speaking at this time.

Meeting-Changer

Most women's groups set up a regular, recurring time and date for their meetings. These dates are usually unchangeable and in this way all members can plan accordingly.

Every so often something comes up unexpectedly with one of your members, and they find out they can't make a scheduled meeting. There are two ways to handle this. Either she simply misses the planned meeting or the meeting date can be changed by the group as a whole.

In our group, which is an easily manageable size, we usually attempt to accommodate our member if there's enough time beforehand to change the meeting and let everyone know. Our rule is – if you can't make the meeting, you are responsible for contacting everyone, getting their agreement on a mutually acceptable replacement date and making sure everyone is alerted to the final plans. This is the Meeting-Changer and that responsibility only arises as an exception.

Fixed (or Permanent) Roles

Fixed roles are those which don't change from meeting to meeting. Usually someone who likes taking on a specific responsibility will volunteer to perform a permanent role. Most times, someone steps up to take on a role that is easy or comfortable for them to perform.

Treasurer

Women's groups don't necessarily need a President, Vice President or Secretary because these groups tend to be less formal than a true club. But there's always a need for someone to collect funds for a specific event and handle monetary issues within your group. That's the job of the Treasurer.

If there's a birthday present to be purchased, money to be collected for a group trip, or a payment to be made to a guest speaker, someone has to be responsible for taking care of this. Some groups may choose to have dues and if so, the Treasurer will keep a ledger of who has paid and who has not.

Calendar Keeper

One person needs to keep track of whose turn it is to host the next meeting, where it will be and when. This person is responsible for making sure the group discusses the next meeting before the current meeting ends. It is typically part of the closing ritual.

We have found if the next meeting is not planned while everyone is in the same room, it's very hard to get everyone to agree to when it will be held. It requires all sorts of phone calls and emails to make it happen. For simplicity sake, make your plans when you're all together.

> For simplicity sake, make your plans when you're all together.

You may decide that the Calendar Keeper is to send an email to each group member as a reminder a few days before the next meeting is to be held.

Dining-Out Diva

Whenever your group goes to a restaurant for a meeting or an "extracurricular" birthday or anniversary party, there will be a check to be figured out. Unless each member receives her own check, there's a problem in divvying up the bill. So, try to be fair to everyone. Ask that everyone not quibble about pennies.

It is up to the Dining-Out Diva to make sure the check-figuring is done correctly. She will calculate an appropriate tip, add it into the check, split the amount evenly among the group, tell everyone what they are responsible for and collect the funds. There's always one in your group who will be adept at taking care of this readily, which makes it easier on everyone else.

> *Usually we split the bill evenly, provided that everyone has had a similar meal. In our group we have some women who like a few glasses of wine with their meal and others who don't. So we separate out the bar bill from the meal and split that evenly between the wine-lovers. Of course if one person has had much more food or drink than all the others, we are respectful of each other's needs and that person will offer to throw in some extra cash to cover her expenditure. And if the restaurant will allow you to have separate checks, all the better!*

<u>Event Organizer</u>

This member is in charge of coordinating group celebrations, such as birthdays and outings. Much like the Calendar Keeper, any celebration has to be planned ahead of time and, if possible, should be planned as part of the closing ritual of your meeting.

The celebration must be put on the calendar, a location must be chosen, and if there's to be carpooling, that has to be considered too. If your group is larger than four and you're intending to go to a restaurant, the Event Organizer should make a reservation. She may also have to do some emailing in order to take care of the details, and of course if your celebration is to be a surprise for one of the members, your organizer will have to be discreet. An email reminder should be sent to each member a few days before the celebration.

Whom Do I Invite?

> *A dream you dream alone is only a dream.*
> *A dream you dream together is reality.*
>
> –JOHN LENNON

Deciding whom to invite to your group is a process that takes some thought.

At first glance it might be fun to gather together a bunch of your friends. They would probably say "yes" to your invite and would come to see what it's all about. It would be easy to talk to them and get them involved. They might truly enjoy this opportunity to add something to their lives, or they might just be humoring you. They might support you all the way in your new endeavor, or they might just come to one or two meetings to be polite and never come back.

So let's think about it. Do you think all your friends would be the right members for your group? What if they don't all get along? What if they don't want to follow your guidelines? Couldn't this get in the way of a good friendship? And what if you leave someone out? Inviting friends can have its difficulties too.

There are other choices for whom to invite. You could place a notice up at your child's school or afterschool activity; you could pass the word around at your place of worship; you could even advertise for interested members on the internet using any number of women-related websites or blogs to find members. All of these options would get you a group of strangers, a group of people who may have seen each other before but don't know each other well or at all. This can lead to some challenges in weeding out whom is right for your group, but it's another way to gather a grouping to select from.

In either case, you can assume that some of the people who start out coming to your group will stay and participate fully, others will come for a short time and move on, and others will not express an interest in continuing with the group after the first or second meeting. You can expect it all.

What Makes a Good Choice of a Person?

There are many characteristics that go into a person's makeup. Some traits are more important than others when you think of who might be a good group member. Depending on the type of group you are starting, you may find yourself drawn to people with some, but not all, of the

> Without honesty,
> the talk is just talk.

following characteristics. See which characteristics jive with your idea of the type of people you want in your group.

Honesty

Truthfulness and sincerity help the group get to know you and to learn to trust you. One may fear that being honest may open one up to ridicule, but without honesty, the talk is just talk.

Intelligence

Smart people can be deep thinkers. They have a capacity for learning, reasoning and understanding. They can see issues from many different sides at once.

Openness

Openness takes on many meanings. The ability to be receptive to new ideas and suggestions without prejudging allows for personal growth. Being open to change is the ability to embrace change as it comes into one's life rather than simply enduring it. New concepts will be explored in your meetings, and having members who are able to "go with the flow" is a plus.

Being open-minded requires a person who is receptive and interested in the opinions and ideas of others without being prejudiced or bigoted. This person makes both a good listener and a welcome participant.

Creativity

A creative thinker can transcend traditional ideas and rules and bring new and meaningful ideas to the table. Imaginative thought takes many forms – writing, painting, music, movement, problem solving – all of which contribute to a successful group.

Interest

An interesting person has something new and different to say, has thoughts that come from her varied experiences, and can be entertaining to listen to.

Curiosity

Inquisitive, eager to learn people are ones who want to experience everything they have never tried before. They are able to jump right in and participate.

Willingness to Learn and Grow

An interest in acquiring knowledge or learning a new skill makes one an active participant.

Optimism

A person who has a general sense of positive feelings and thoughts is able to contribute to the group in a constructive, hopeful fashion; whereas, a negative person tends to bring down the other members of the group with her lack of optimism.

Trustworthiness

One who is dependable and reliable can be counted on to keep the group's private discussions to herself and not tell tales about the other members within the group.

Ability to Share

Women who can relate a personal experience or share a secret with others keep the group's conversation moving. Bringing ones thoughts, feelings, and dreams into the mix enhances her importance to the group.

Respect of Others

The ability to assert ones opinions while being compassionate toward others takes into consideration the feelings of everyone in the group. One's ideas can be distinct and well formulated but still presented in a respectful fashion so as not to alienate other members.

What Are Your Criteria For Group Members?

There are many reasons for organizing a women's group and many combinations of types of women you might want to include. Think about the criteria that makes sense to you.

Age or Stage

Some groups are made up of people who are all around the same age. This would be true for a group of "young professionals," "forties fun," or "retirement living." These groups include those who are in a specific decade of life.

Other women's groups center around a particular stage of life such as "new moms," where what is in common is the fact that all members have new babies, not that they are the same age. In this group, one might find both a 20 year old and a 40 year old who have lots in common even though they differ in age.

The success and longevity of our group is based on many factors. We came together when we were in our mid-forties at a time when we were mature enough to appreciate what other women had to offer to each of us. We accepted each other without being judgmental or fearful of being criticized for our own shortcomings. We were able to learn to be open to each other in the safety of the group setting, talk with clarity and honest emotion, and accept each person for what she brought to the table.

Groups where women share a common hobby or love of an activity may have no appropriate age or stage. Anyone wanting to share that activity would be welcome. It's wonderful to learn from others who have more or less experience than you do.

Similarity or Diversity

Do you want everyone to come from the same background, or do you prefer varied histories? Should they all have grown up in the same area of the country or all come from completely different beginnings? Should they all belong to a gym or is it unimportant how they feel about staying in shape? What is it that brings your group members together?

> Creating a group with women who are different from you is a broadening experience and having women in the group who would not ordinarily be in your life is exciting and stimulating.

A group that is more "homogeneous" is one that is composed of women who are all of the same kind or nature. They are similar to one another, essentially alike in some dimension. That doesn't mean your group will be uninteresting. On the contrary! When a group that shares many traits comes together, they tend to be comfortable and it's easy to understand what others are saying when you've had similar experiences in your own life. These groups can solidify very quickly.

A group that is more "heterogeneous" is one that is composed of women with widely varied characteristics or diverse backgrounds. Creating a group with women who are different from you is a broadening experience and having women in the group who would not ordinarily be in your life is exciting and stimulating. Think of how many new ideas will arise in such a diverse group.

Specifically think about similarities or diversity in regard to the following:

- geographical background
- race
- temperament
- socioeconomic status
- religious background
- level of education

Our women's group is comprised of a group of women who are all in a similar age group (seven years between youngest and oldest member). We all hail from the east coast of the United States, and we all have similar political views. We have similar levels of advanced education and similar feelings about child-rearing and dealing with teens. And we all love to dine in restaurants with friends. So we tend to be homogeneous.

But within our group of similar-type individuals, we have enormous differences. Some of us laugh freely, and others are more serious. Some of us have been married. Most (but not all) have grown children. Some of us are in relationships and some are not; some are more spiritual, practical, ethereal or down to earth. Some have worked as professionals for many years, and some have been stay-at-home moms. Some cry easily, and others hold their feelings in check. The list of similarities and differences goes on and on, even within our group.

<u>Choose a Theme for Inviting</u>

So much to think about! If you don't have a specific direction to go in, select a theme to help you decide who to invite. This will help you narrow down the choices. Even if you're placing an ad online or on a bulletin board, phrase it in such a way as to attract the type of people you're looking for.

Simple themes to go with are:

- People I know (friends, co-workers, members of a club)
- A shared situation (women in transition, single parents, workaholics, mothers and daughters)
- One age group (thirty-somethings, young moms, over-the-hill'ers)
- Similar background (same religion, daughters of farmers, city-folk, same ethnic group)
- Shared hobby or passion (avid readers, prayer group, problem solving group, activity group, those who love to bake)

How Big is Just Right?

The perfect number of people for your group depends on what type of group you are starting, where you will be able to meet, and what the goals are.

> If there are too many members, there isn't enough time and space for each individual to express herself adequately.

Limiting the number of people in your group is a good thing. If there are too many members, there isn't enough time and space for each individual to express herself adequately. If there are too few, the conversation may not be stimulating enough and the flow of ideas won't be as broad. Also, too few may simply turn into an informal coffee klatch, which may be fun but is not the point of forming this group.

We suggest five to fifteen people as the right number of members to strive for. Five or six may be just the right number for a group that wants to delve deeply into a topic in detail, allowing each person a longer time to speak. With twelve to fifteen women, you will have to keep track of how long each person is talking and make sure everyone has a fair chance to participate.

The group Pat started is a closed group, and we have found that eight is the perfect number for us. It is intimate yet large enough to get a good cross section of opinions and ideas. We each get multiple chances to talk, and we can even pair off for an activity leaving no one out. When we go out to an event, we can fit into two cars easily and if we share a meal at a restaurant, eight can sit comfortably around a table and still hear each other.

At the beginning, you may want to invite more people than you expect to be in the group permanently because, most likely, not everyone will decide to join. The first two or three meetings will have different attendees, and allowing a flexible number will ensure you get a group together.

If you intend to be a closed group, once you have your target number of people committed to joining, you should close your group to newcomers. Later on in the life of your group some members may leave. At that time you can add new women to replace them or decide as a group to stay at the smaller size. You can also decide to enlarge the group at any time if it meets the needs of all your members.

Extend the Invitation

All life is an experiment.
The more experiments you make the better.

—Ralph Waldo Emerson

There are many ways to extend an invitation to a potential member. Whether you call someone on the phone, invite her in person or send an email, there are a few approaches that work well. They are general in nature, short and sweet with just enough of a teaser to pique her curiosity.

There are four sections to the invitation:

The Lead -- The Detail -- The Ask – The Bring-Along

The Lead

This is your opening line. It says what you're trying to accomplish in *one* simple sentence.

> ### The Lead
> In one sentence, say what you're trying to accomplish.

- "I'm hosting an evening for women where we'll get together and explore interesting issues."
- "I'm starting a group for women where we'll learn to live our lives to the fullest."
- "I'm hosting a parenting group to discuss issues relating to moms and their kids."
- "I'm interested in starting a women's group where we might learn some new things about ourselves and each other."
- "I'm gathering a group of women that want to grow and develop a stronger spiritual life."
- "I'm bringing together a group of women who are looking to add more fun into their lives."
- "I'm starting a 'women only' book club."

The Detail

> ### The Detail
> A little bit of information about what they can expect.

Here is where you give a small bit of additional information as to what they can expect at your get-together, making sure to impress upon them that there will be no pressure on them to participate or perform.

- "It will be fun and relaxing."
- "There'll be some chatting and small group activities with no pressure."
- "There'll be meetings and outside experiences."
- "I'd like to make some new friendships that could last a lifetime."
- "It'll be a watch and learn evening."
- "We'll share recipes and then make dinner right there."
- "We'll read a book before the meeting and discuss important points or ideas that struck us as interesting."

The Ask

It is important to clearly ask for their participation. No beating around the bush! Ask for it and you'll get an answer. If you never ask, they may hem and haw and not take you seriously.

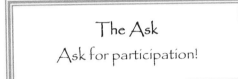

The Ask
Ask for participation!

- "Would you be interested?"
- "Do you think you can make it?"
- "Would you like to join us?"
- "Can I count you in?"

The Bring-Along

This section is very important. Here is where you ask them if they know anyone else they'd like to come with. Many women will feel more comfortable attending your women's group if they are able to come with a friend. And for you as you get started, the more the merrier!

The Bring-Along
Invite them to bring a friend.

- "Who else do you know who might be willing to join us in starting a women's group?"
- "Is there anyone else you'd like to bring with you?"
- "You're welcome to bring along a friend."
- "Do you know someone else who'd be up for a new experience?"

- "Is there someone you'd be comfortable asking to join us?"

Here's a complete sample invitation that will do the trick:

> *"I'm hosting an evening for women to get together where we'll explore interesting issues.*
> *It will be fun and relaxing.*
> *Would you be interested?*
> *Who else do you know who might be willing to join us in starting a group?"*

You're sure to get some "yes" answers with this easy invite. Do remember that even after they accept your invitation, some women may cancel. Maybe they have a date or time conflict they forgot about. Possibly they've thought it over and are hesitant to attend, and maybe they just have no idea of the opportunity they're missing. But keep in mind, it's never personal.

If you're placing an advertisement or a putting a notice up on a bulletin board, the same holds true. Be general in nature, pique someone's curiosity, and be sure to include your phone number or email so individuals can contact you directly. Do not put up a notice announcing where and when the meeting will be. You do not want to have too many people showing up unannounced.

> Some women may cancel.
> Maybe they just have no idea
> of the opportunity
> they're missing.

For people you do not know, you do want to speak to each one briefly to try to make sure they are a good fit for your group. Feel them out a bit. You can give them some information, but if they're a complete stranger, you should not hold your meeting at home. Instead, plan your meeting in a public setting, like a restaurant or meeting room, until you're comfortable with the people attending the meetings. You'll know quickly enough whether it's appropriate to start holding the meetings in someone's home.

Let's Get Down to Setting Up

Simple preparation ahead of time will allow your meeting to flow. You should think about these things initially and prepare ahead of time for your first few meetings. Later these choices will be discussed and decided upon by all the members of your group.

To Feed or Not to Feed

Do you want to serve food as a part of your meetings? Food nurtures the soul, fortifies us during heavy discussions and refreshes us after a fantastic get-together. It's not mandatory, but it's a nice touch.

> Food nurtures the soul, fortifies us during heavy discussions and refreshes us after a fantastic get-together.

If you're including refreshments in your meetings, you need to decide what to serve. Will you have simple snacks or a full meal? Will there be munchies, a light buffet, desserts only or a sit-down meal? Will the Hostess pay for the food or should there be a potluck meal where everyone contributes a dish?

It is the Hostess's choice to decide, and for the first few meetings, Ms. Visionary, it's your show! Keep it simple to begin with as you will be leading the meeting and can't be running back and forth to the kitchen to check the oven and serve.

There's a wide variety of easy-to-prepare and easy-to-eat snacks. Depending on the local customs in your area, find something your group would be familiar with and enjoy.

Also take into consideration your audience. If your group is made up of moms who have young children, they might appreciate a nice glass (or two!) of wine to go along with their very adult-only meeting. If your group is all about being healthy, fresh veggies or a nice fruit salad might be most appropriate. If your group is meeting after dinner, it would make sense to have dessert and coffee. No matter what you choose, water should be available to all throughout the meeting.

Some good choices are:

• Chips and salsa	• Fruit and chocolates
• Wine and cheese	• Ice cream
• Coffee and cake	• Pizza
• Cookies and milk	• Chinese takeout
• Fresh veggies and dip	• Potluck dinner

Over the years, our women's group has had a few different visions of what to serve. First we had light snacks, soda and coffee. But our meetings were being held in the evenings after work, and our members didn't have time to eat dinner before the meeting. One by one they started bringing take-out food with them.

So we decided to serve a simple dinner as part of the meeting, buffet style with our plates on our laps. That worked nicely for quite some time, even though it did tend to get in the way of our topic discussion.

To simplify and formalize the process, we started having dinner around the dining room table. That was certainly nice, but our hostesses felt obliged to serve something pre-dinner as the women were gathering, so now we added finger food, cheese and crackers and the like to the before-dinner section of our meeting. You see where I'm going?

The dinners eventually became more and more elaborate. Yes, it was easy to have our meeting around the table, but our meetings began to be more about the food than about the topic! So we have now removed the hors d' oeuvres, simplified the dinner and brought the topic back into the forefront. Much better.

Set the Mood

Whether your meetings are held in your home, at a café or in a conference space, you want your guests to feel an instant level of comfort. Think about the mood you want to set and create it.

At home, some soft-smelling candles, essential oils or incense along with soothing background music will instantly set a calm tone and promote relaxation. Flowers always make people feel comfortable too. After all, everyone will be coming to an unfamiliar setting and will be both excited and a bit uneasy or apprehensive.

> Create a quiet space where there won't be interruptions from family or pets.

Create a quiet space where there won't be interruptions from family or pets. We have found that a circle of chairs or comfortable furniture is the best arrangement so everyone can see each other and feel equal to all others in the room. In other words, no one is sitting at the head of a table or in front of the room like a teacher.

If your meeting is being held in a more public space, you may have to adapt to the surroundings as they are. In a restaurant, try to find a round table. Place your symbolic candles or flowers in the center.

If you are in a plain or unexciting public room with chairs for your use, don't forget the circle arrangement so all members are facing each other. Make sure it's large enough for all the members, but not too big, which could hinder group discussion. You want to create a just-the-right-size grouping of people. A small central table can hold your candle or flowers and act as a focal point.

Scheduling

How often do you think you'd want to meet? Once a month, once a week? Depending on the type of group you are starting, the frequency of meetings will vary. A mommies group might want to meet every week, a book club or self-help group might prefer monthly meetings.

> Think about the best way to ensure continued participation and always remember that whatever you start with doesn't have to be the way it goes forever.

What day of the week will your meetings be? Is it better to be during the week so as not to interfere with everyone's weekend and family obligations? Or would a Sunday afternoon be preferable because everyone works Monday through Friday and will be able to look forward to a nice afternoon spent together? Should it be an evening meeting, afternoon get-together, morning rise and shine group?

There is no right or wrong here, it is your choice.

Think about what would be the best way to ensure continued participation and always remember that whatever you start with doesn't have to be the way it goes forever. Once your group has come together, you will all choose a day, time, and frequency to meet all your needs.

Time Frame

How long should your meeting be? Long enough to satisfy your members and short enough to keep them wanting to come back for more.

Certainly it shouldn't be less than an hour and probably shouldn't take up an entire afternoon or evening, but this too depends on the amount of people, level of involvement, and activities you are planning.

We have found that a meeting in someone's home when food is served or at a restaurant should last about two and a half to three hours. This length seems to be just right. No one gets bored or tired of sitting, and if our conversation is hopping, sometimes the meeting extends way beyond that time – but at a more informal level.

Meeting Place

Where to hold your meetings depends on how many people you plan to have, whether you already know them, and what's generally available and comfortable for the members of your group.

You can choose a public venue such as a restaurant or diner where you can have a large round table in a corner or private room. Here the food part is taken care of by someone else, which is very nice, but it also will cost your members money. Consider the fact that you're asking people to spend money to attend your meetings. This may be an issue.

You can meet at a club house, a country club or a meeting room in a hotel or motel. Here you'll have to make sure that comfortable seating and easy access to any refreshments you provide is available.

It's always nice to meet at a more intimate location, such as your home. Provided your space is large enough to handle the group you're inviting, it is easier for all your guests to simply come and participate without having to worry about any discomfort in being in a public place or dealing with any possible expense. Of course it's a bit more stressful for you because now you're not only the Visionary and the Topic Presenter, but the Hostess too!

To hold the meeting at your home, you have to find a private area where you won't be disturbed by family members or pets. What if your husband or children are also at home? How do your guests speak freely when people external to the group may hear what they say?

We found it was best if other family members could leave the house while our meeting was going on. Of course, our children were older and could occupy themselves at a friend's house or be out for a few hours in the evening.

We did tend to kick out the men in our lives when possible as it's quite hard to be discussing women's issues when you know there are curious ears listening in the background.

If you have young children you may want to hire a baby sitter to watch them while you're hosting the group.

If the meetings are comfortable in members' homes, we suggest rotating houses among the members. In this way everyone becomes the Hostess at some point. And, if there are eight people in your group, you'll only have to have it at your house once every eight meetings.

Not a bad deal.

> If the meetings are comfortable
> in members' homes,
> we suggest rotating houses
> among the members.

If someone is not comfortable hosting a meeting, work around them. This shouldn't be a reason that keeps them from joining in the group. Their personal situation at home may not be conducive to having a group of women descend upon the household.

Since there is an expense for each Hostess when it's her turn, this member might contribute a dessert, bottle of wine or a specified amount of cash to Hostesses to help in sharing the cost even though she's not hosting herself.

Group Info Card

This is a great addition to give out to your potential members.

We strongly suggest you create a Group Information Card to hand out to your members at their first meeting. It can be business card sized so they can carry it in their wallets or it can be larger – something they can place on their bulletin boards at home. This will give them something to think about and remember for future meetings.

Include the following:

Your Name

Your Contact Info (email, phone)

Purpose of your Women's Group

Our Group Success Practices –

- Everyone is to be treated with respect

- All ideas are welcomed and there are no right or wrong ideas

- One person talks at a time

- Practice listening as well as speaking

- Confidentiality is crucial

For a detailed description of our suggested Rules of the Road, see Chapter 7 – *Organize the First Meeting.*

What If Nobody Likes My Vision?

> *All our dreams can come true if we have*
> *the courage to pursue them.*
>
> -WALT DISNEY

So, now you've thought of everything. You've got a good idea of what your meeting will include and a decent feel for what you want to accomplish. You know where it will be and when. You'll provide snacks and coffee. You've asked a group of women to join you and enough have said yes. You've got a small shopping list of things to buy – some candles, a new music CD. You're ready.

And now there's doubt. What if nobody likes my vision when they come to the first meeting? What if no one shows up? What if I can't make the meeting work? What if it's a disaster?

It is certainly a big undertaking to think about starting a women's group. You know that, yet you're going to do it. You have all the tools and guidance you need right here. If you follow our suggestions for your first meeting, you will be sure to have success. That doesn't mean everything will be perfect. We can't assure you of that. You will do your best, your guests will do their best, and you'll take it as it comes.

Preparation ahead of time on your part will make your meeting flow. You'll always have a next step and a next activity to get to. Your level of excitement and commitment will be transmitted to your guests.

If you're enjoying yourself and the process, they will too. You'll be amazed at how many ideas they will contribute to the group. Who knows where your vision will end up? That's the fun of it all.

Let's Recap: *How Do I Get Started?*

In order to start a group, follow these basic steps:

1. Choose a focus for your meeting.

2. Choose a group type
   a. Closed
   b. Open
   c. Drop-In

3. Establish rules
   a. Listen
   b. Share ownership
   c. Confidentiality is essential
   d. Show up regularly and participate

4. Identify roles
   a. Rotating Roles: Hostess, Facilitator or Topic Presenter, Timekeeper, Meeting-Changer
   b. Fixed Roles: Treasurer, Calendar Keeper, Dining-Out Diva, Event Organizer

5. Choose members
   a. Choose carefully. Friends aren't always the best option.
   b. Decide which attributes and criteria are important to you.
   c. Keep it a manageable size.

6. Invite
   a. Lead with an opening line
   b. Detail: add additional information
   c. Ask
   d. Bring along a friend.

7. Setting up
    a. To feed or not to feed. That is the question.
    b. Set the mood with flowers or candles.
    c. Schedule a time that works for all members.
    d. Select a time frame of an hour or more.
    e. Choose an appropriate meeting place.

8. Be confident. Don't doubt your vision!

Chapter 6: Structure of a Meeting

> *Basic human contact*
> *— the meeting of eyes, the exchanging of words —*
> *is to the psyche what oxygen is to the brain. If you're feeling*
> *abandoned by the world, interact with anyone you can.*
>
> *–MARTHA BECK*

In a society where people keep in touch through Facebook and Twitter, what better opportunity is there to encourage intimacy than during the meeting of minds in a physical place?

Much thought goes into organizing every part of your women's group meeting. From beginning to end, your meeting should flow easily and with proper planning, everything should fall nicely into place.

Here we will help you set the stage and outline a typical meeting from beginning to end. In the following two chapters, we speak about the first two meetings more specifically as there are some extra preparations and details that need to be considered when your women's group first begins.

For now, learn what the overall basic structure of your regularly scheduled meetings should be.

Pre-Planning

Hostessing a women's group meeting takes some thought ahead of time for it to be well-run, welcoming, and compelling. With proper planning, your meetings will be in a comfortable setting, will have an organized beginning-to-end flow, and will meet the needs of your group members so they will want to come back for more.

Select a Topic

The focus of each meeting is the main topic and it is up to the Facilitator or Topic Presenter to decide upon the topic. You, as the Visionary, will select the topic for the first two to four meetings. It will be your job to choose an engaging topic that will be relevant to your members' lives. This topic should be thought-provoking, creative or fun.

> When selecting a topic,
> consider the stated focus or theme of
> your women's group,
> the type of members you're appealing to,
> and even the time of year.

When selecting a Topic, consider the stated focus or theme of your women's group, the type of members you're appealing to and even the time of year (include holiday-related topics where appropriate).

For a detailed selection of topic suggestions, see our associated book entitled "A Topic for Everyone: Women's Group Discussion Topics and Activities".

Gather Tools or Supplies

Some topics may require pencils and paper or magazines, scissors and glue or preprinted handouts with an interesting quote to be pondered or a video to be viewed. These items will be used to stimulate creative thought and discussion.

These tools and supplies should be created or gathered by the Hostess ahead of time, so they'll be available when the group meets.

Decide Upon a Menu

If you're panning to serve food as part of your meeting, you have to decide what you're making and how much time you want to devote to creating a welcoming table.

To be organized, it's best to create a list ahead of time of all the things you'll need for your guests. Include any snack items, appetizers, main dishes, salads, side dishes, desserts, beverages or whatever you plan to serve. Also include plates, cups, napkins, forks and other needed utensils. Better to be prepared than to forget something important like milk for coffee!

Remember that food nurtures the soul, fortifies us during heavy discussions and refreshes us after a fantastic get-together.

And, of course, the day of your meeting will require time for you to prepare your dining choices.

Set the Mood

Whether your meetings are held in your home, at a café, or in a conference space, you want your guests to feel an instant level of comfort. Think about the mood you want to set and create it.

Think about including any or all of the following:

- Candles, essential oils, incense or flowers
- Soothing background music
- Quiet space without interruptions from family or pets
- Soft lighting or strong, bright lights

Prepare the Setting

Remember the power of the circle and see how the circle plays a big role in your meetings.

> Place chairs in a circle,
> not too big and not too small,
> so that all members are facing
> each other.

We strongly suggest placing chairs in a circle, not too big and not too small, so that all members are facing each other. If you're in a living room or den with furniture already set up, do your best to have people sitting in a circular arrangement. It centers your group, allowing everyone to see each other easily. No one is left out. In this way, all members have an equal place in your setting.

Choose a Length of Time

Certainly your meeting shouldn't be less than an hour and probably shouldn't take up an entire afternoon or evening, but this too depends on the amount of people, level of involvement and type of activities you are planning.

We have found two and a half hours works quite well for us, including relaxing around the food served. It should be long enough to fit in all the elements that are important, but not long enough where your group is yawning or checking their watches repeatedly. You always want to leave them wanting a bit more.

For most meetings with a featured topic and some sort of food being served, two to two and a half hours is a good starting point. Check out our outline below for a standard two and a half hour women's group meeting.

From Beginning to End

Opening the Meeting (30 minutes)

Put Out the Welcome Mat

Welcome each guest as she arrives. Introduce yourself to anyone who doesn't already know you or is new to the meeting. Guide your guests to a seat and make them feel comfortable. Allow everyone to chat informally while you're waiting for others to show up. You can be sure that women will have no trouble making small talk.

Starting Ritual

Once everyone has arrived, you should start the meeting. If there's music on, you may want to turn it off. If the lights are bright, you may want to lower them; if they are low, try turning them up. All of these things will alert everyone that the meeting is about to begin. Have everyone find a seat.

Some groups have a Starting Ritual at the beginning of each meeting. It might be the lighting of a candle, saying a prayer, taking some deep breaths, performing a one-minute meditation, doing some simple stretches, closing one's eyes and focusing or just saying hi to each member of the group.

Announcements

As the Hostess, you may have some announcements to make to the group as a whole. Now is the time to get any formalities out of the way. If someone has given their regrets and is not coming, if someone needs a ride home or if there's a storm approaching and you're planning to end early – these are all things to announce at this time.

Time to Catch Up

When women get together, they always want to catch up with each other and hear any personal news. It's very natural to want to know what's been happening with others at the meeting, especially if you haven't seen them since the last meeting. After all, that could be a month ago, and that's a long time.

We have found it's best to let everyone have a chance to relate any exciting or important news to the group at the beginning of the meeting. In this way, you'll minimize side chatter during the formal portion of the meeting.

> When women get together, they always want to catch up with each other and hear any personal news.

The Hostess should start by holding the talking object, giving a two minute synopsis of anything personal she'd like to present to the group and then passing it (along with the right to speak) to the next person.

Go around the room so that everyone has a chance to catch the group up with their latest happenings. If you have a Timekeeper, she should watch the time, remember to move the conversation along, gently remind someone to wrap up where needed, and keep the talking object moving.

The Meat of the Meeting (1 ¾ hours)

This section of your meeting is the core, and we are presenting it as one long section rather than breaking it into its two components: Featured Topic Presentation and Let There Be Food.

Some groups will present their Featured Topic at this time and spend an hour or more on it and then choose to have snacks, munchies or a full meal afterward. Other groups will serve an eat-on-your-lap meal first, allow for informal chat, clear the dishes and then present the Featured Topic. Some groups choose to have nibbles all the way through the meeting and not break for any major food presentation. And others may not include any food at all. Drinks should always be available, whether it is soda and juice, coffee and tea, beer or wine, or simply water.

Featured Topic Presentation

This is the main focus of the meeting. The Hostess has decided on the topic and presents it to the group along with any of the ready to use tools and supplies that may be needed. Sometimes it is fun to give out the tools or supplies first while no one knows what is coming next. It helps ramp up the excitement level.

If your group has separated the Hostessing from the Topic Presenter duties, then the latter should be introduced and take center stage. At this point, it's all her show.

Most of our topics are things to talk about and don't require any tools or supplies. So when our Hostess comes over to the circle with scissors in hand, paper and pencils or magic markers, we all give that condescending groan to her. We all feel like we're in school and we sit up straight and get ready for "the assignment." It always turns out to be something very creative and fun to do, so we all end up quite pleased after our initial apprehension.

The topic can be something controversial to discuss or something that lights a fire in each of us such as:

> "How do you remember to take care of YOU each and every day?
> And how does your family support you – or not – in this endeavor?"

Let everyone mull this over for a minute or two before asking who wants to speak first. Pass the talking object to the first volunteer and let her speak for three to four minutes. Go around the room and give everyone a chance to contribute their thoughts. This will allow even the quiet or hesitant women to have a say.

Everyone should be encouraged to contribute, however small it might be. If you have a Timekeeper, she should watch the time, remember to move the conversation along, gently remind someone to wrap up where needed and keep the talking object moving. It is important to note that the Timekeeper must also be sensitive to each individual woman's situation. There are times when a woman is sharing and will need more time. At the same time, the Timekeeper must be sure one person does not monopolize the time.

Going around the room is important so that everyone gets a chance to speak. If you randomly pass the talking object to the next person who has raised their hand or who is jumping up and down, the more vocal members at your meeting will do most of the talking. And the quiet members will get easily overlooked while hiding quietly trying not to take the floor. It is necessary to make sure everyone has a chance to participate so no one is left out.

If there's time, go around the room more than once. You can be sure your talkers will certainly want to speak more than once! And if only some people want to speak the second time around, let them each have the talking object and chat away.

The topic can also be an activity where you hand out pencils and paper and ask everyone to:

"List ten things you want to accomplish by the end of the year."

Give everyone five minutes to write down their ten goals. If some people are having trouble coming up with all ten, you can make a few suggestions. Remind them that not everything has to be a big thing. Something like "getting a pedicure" or "having a massage" is every bit as important a goal as "asking for a raise" or "losing ten pounds."

When everyone is done, ask who wants to speak first. Pass the talking object to her and have her read her list. There'll be plenty of nodding in agreement, chuckling and "oh yeah, I forgot that one" coming from your guests. When she's done, have her pass the talking object to the next person and go around the room with everyone's lists.

There'll be time to go around the room more than once, discussing the pros and cons of some of the entries. Once they've all been read, ask for a consensus on the group's three favorites.

Another suggested activity for groups that have been together for awhile or who know each other well is as follows: the Topic Presenter will give each person a pencil and one small piece of paper or index card for each other member in the group. If there are eight attendees, everyone gets seven pieces of paper. Have each person write one guest's name down on each piece of paper. Then they are instructed to:

"Write down one positive trait about each person in the room."

Give everyone a chance to finish this activity and then come together as a group. It's important with this activity that no one knows who said what about whom!

Have everyone separate their papers into a pile for each person. The Topic Presenter will then hand a pile to each member in the group, making sure no one has gotten the pile that is about her. Go around the room and have each member announce who they're reading and read all the comments about that person.

> How great it is to know how you are perceived in a positive light.

This can be one of the most wonderful activities for a group to share. Each participant comes away feeling good about herself and knowing someone in the room has said these affirming, positive things about her. All negativity is removed from this experience. How great it is to know how you are perceived in a positive light.

To finish, you can pass the talking object, go around the circle discussing feelings or patterns that were identified, discussing positive vs. negative thoughts or anything that comes to mind as a follow-up to this activity.

<u>Let There Be Food</u>

As the Hostess, you have decided upon a menu, and you have chosen whether your fare will be served before, during or after the Featured Topic Presentation.

Snacks or hors d'oeuvres can easily be set out at the onset of the meeting so your guests can munch as everyone is arriving and catching up. They shouldn't get in the way of any opening conversation. Soft drinks, wine or juice can also be available at this time as well.

Similarly, serving coffee and tea, cake, ice cream or another dessert at the end of a meeting makes it easy for everyone to serve themselves. This also shouldn't get in the way of any closing activities. Many women enjoy ending the meeting with a nice cup of coffee to finish things off. It represents the end of a good meal or the end of a good meeting.

If you are including a sit down lunch, brunch or dinner or a buffet table as part of your gathering, you have to decide when to serve.

If your group meets in the evening after work, it may be appropriate to serve your meal before the Featured Topic Presentation as everyone is hungry and tired from a long day. This will serve to perk everyone up. Just make sure you don't dwell on the meal too long; otherwise, you won't have enough time for a thorough topic discussion. Once the meal is over, your group can return to the circle and start the topic.

If you prefer to have your Featured Topic presented before the meal, you will have everyone's attention during your discussion because they are ready to participate at the get-go and they know they will be rewarded with a feast afterward! This can be good to use for brunch or a luncheon meeting if you time it right. Possibly an 11 AM meeting with coffee served at the start would work well because you can serve brunch or lunch at about 12:30, just when everyone's stomach begins to grumble.

Some groups will choose to have their Featured Topic Presentation coincide with the meal. Lunch or dinner can be served. When people are halfway through or finishing up with the main course and before dessert or coffee, the Hostess can present the topic. Everyone can mull it over for a minute or two and then remain at the dining table for a hearty discussion.

Hand the talking object to the first speaker and get the discussion going. Dessert and coffee or tea can then be served, and we all know how easy it is to chat with others while relaxing over a hot cup of tea. We women have no problem with this scenario. Your discussion or activity will be well received by all.

Closing the Meeting (15 minutes)

A formal closing of your meeting allows your guests to reflect on what happened during the current meeting and sets the stage for your next meeting.

Remember to thank everyone for coming and sharing. Make sure they know how happy you are that they have joined you this evening.

Discuss the particulars of the next meeting. Ask everyone to take out their calendars so the next date and location can be set up. Here's where the Calendar Keeper is queen. It is up to her to know whose turn it is to be Hostess and if you have a separate Topic Presenter, she will alert the group as to whose turn it is for presenting. Once a date is agreed on, she will put the next meeting on the calendar and be responsible for emailing everyone a reminder a few days before the next meeting is scheduled.

> Remember to thank everyone for coming and sharing.

In addition, if there are any birthday or holiday celebrations coming up, your Calendar Keeper and Event Organizer will work together to help you get any of these extracurricular activities on the calendar and reserved. We always look forward to sharing celebrations together.

Just like your opening routine has a starting ritual, you may choose to establish a closing ritual. This would include blowing out your ceremonial candle, a few moments of meditation, a squeeze of the hand or a hearty hug for each member. Sometimes simply wishing everyone a good weekend, week or month is enough.

Many times you will find that the closing ritual comes naturally; you may not need to create a formal one for your members.

Cleanup

Once everyone has left, sit down, take a breath and relax! Notice how your vision is blossoming. Take some time to reflect on the meeting – both good parts and those that need some work.

Write down your thoughts before you forget them. Capture the feelings as they happen. They will be something you can review later when you plan your next get-together.

And some items might be put on the announcement list to present to the group at the next meeting. There's always room for improvement and growth.

Your group needs to be carefully nourished to stay healthy and solid.

Let's Recap: Structure of a Meeting

See how much you can remember from this chapter by answering the following questions:

1. What are four procedures you should do at the beginning of each meeting?
2. What are the two parts to the main meeting — what we called the "Meat of the Meeting"?
3. What role will refreshments play in your group meeting?

ACTION STEP: Now, create a list of ten topics you could discuss at your first few meetings. Be creative and let your thoughts go everywhere!

CHAPTER 6

Chapter 7: Organize the First Meeting

> *Each friend represents a world in us, a world not born until they arrive, and it is only by this meeting that a new world is born.*
>
> –ANAIS NIN

Create Your Vision of the Group

You have been successful in gathering a group of women together, and now you are facilitating the first meeting. It's important to keep your vision in front of the group since you will probably be the leader for the first few months.

You chose the date, time and the place for this meeting and extended the invitation to potential members. Right now the group is all yours, so you get to control these pieces, along with the actual structure of the first meeting. Later on the group as a whole will

> Hold your vision for the group and be open to discussion with other members who may want to implement changes and make improvements.

decide how often to meet, afternoon or evening, weekday or weekend, and the type of location.

In this way, the group will eventually morph into what all of the members want, but for now you are the leader, the one who started the ball rolling, and it's your show. Hold your vision for the group and be open to discussion with other members who may want to implement changes and make improvements.

You should expect your first meeting to last somewhere around two to two and a half hours. It will follow the general Structure of a Meeting (see Chapter 6), but there are some very important items that must be taken care of at this first meeting. You have to introduce yourself, speak of your goals, let your guests introduce themselves, and give your guests the basic ground rules before getting to the featured topic of the meeting.

> Your first meeting will be an eye-opener to you.

For now, let's concentrate on getting started. Your first meeting will be an eye-opener if you remember these tips.

Set the Mood

The first meeting should convey a sense of "no pressure" to your guests. After all, this will be the first time some of them have ever participated in a group of any kind. It may be a bit scary for them. They may be sitting in a room filled with strangers, wondering if they even should have come. Keep the meeting light and present calm surroundings to set everyone at ease.

Decide on any mood assistance you may want like music or scents, and decide where you will locate. Wherever you choose, remember to create a circle so all members can see each other easily.

Introduce Yourself (10 minutes)

The First Meeting is *your* meeting. You are the only one who knows why everyone has been gathered together and what is to come, so it's up to you to be the lead.

Sometimes you know everyone in the room because you have invited a group of friends or neighbors. Other times your attendees will have come because they heard about your group from an ad you placed at your local school, library, or online.

> Steps to the introduction:
> 1. Say who you are.
> 2. Share your reasons for starting the group.
> 3. Discuss the value of female friendships.
> 4. Introduce the talking object.

Your introduction should be long enough to include all of the points listed below, but shouldn't be long-winded either. Sometimes it's hard to judge just where that right time limit is. We suggest keeping your introduction to ten minutes. You've got a lot to say, but don't want it to seem like you are giving a lecture.

Start out by saying who you are

Along with your name, depending on the type of group you have gathered, you might want to say something about your personal life, your family, your job, your age, where you live, your dreams, your ideals. Not too much, but just enough for everyone to get a general feeling about who you are.

Share your reasons for starting the group

Remember, you're the Visionary. This is your group. Tell everyone why you wanted to start a group, why you invited everyone to this meeting, and what you hope to get out of it, both short term and long.

Discuss the value and importance of women's relationships

Women are wonderful, thoughtful people who share openly and learn from each other when they feel safe and secure in their surroundings. Women naturally provide support for each other and challenge each other's ideas. Women grow when they have relationships with other women.

Introduce the Talking Object

It is very common for women to get excited during fascinating discussions and this may lead to lots of interruptions, one woman stepping on another's thoughts. Even if we start out going around the room to give everyone a chance to speak, people tend to jump in at the exact moment when an on-target thought occurs.

To combat this potential issue, you should institute the use of a "talking object", a symbol that indicates whose turn it is to speak. Choose an item that is easy to hold and easy to see, such as a decorated stick, a small decorative pillow or cushion, a painted stone or large seashell, or a symbolic statuette. Make sure it's unbreakable!

Tell everyone the holder of this talking object has the floor and is the only one who can speak. All others are listeners and their role is to listen without an agenda. Despite any strong opinions as to what's being said, no one should comment while the holder of the talking object is speaking. Simply listen wholeheartedly.

Once finished, pass the object to the next person signaling that it is this new person's chance to speak. This really helps to control the group in a non-punitive fashion. It's very easy to remind those interrupters to look and see who holds the talking object.

Depending on how many people are at your meeting, you'll have to decide how long the speaker is permitted to talk before giving someone else a turn. A two to four minute limit for each speaker is sufficient. This way the momentum keeps moving and your members get to hear everyone's views. Of course you can go around the room more than once when appropriate.

If you have a Timekeeper, she should keep track of the time, remember to move the conversation along, gently remind someone to wrap up where needed and keep the talking object moving.

Opening Comments and Ice Breakers (30 minutes)

Personal Introductions (10 minutes)

Once you have finished with your introduction, allow each guest to introduce herself. These personal introductions should be short and sweet – one's name, where she's from, something about herself, and how or why she came to attend this meeting.

We suggest a one to two minute time limit for each guest. This is a great time to practice using the talking object. Everyone will smile as it's passed to them, and they get a chance to have the floor. It's their personal invitation.

You may find that some guests are reluctant to say anything about themselves. That's ok and it's expected. After all, this may be a room full of strangers and that can be very off-putting. You may prompt them with a simple question or two, but let them participate at their own comfort level at the beginning. They'll become more engaged as time goes on.

Ice Breakers (10-20 minutes)

An ice breaker is an opening remark, action, or activity that is designed to ease tension or relieve formality. It's a way to get people to start talking without worrying about saying the wrong thing or being foolish.

There are many commonly used ice breakers that can help to relax a new group of people. You might want to use one to lighten up the mood, once again going around the room. Whenever you plan to give everyone a chance to speak in an orderly fashion, you need to pass the talking object.

A simple non-threatening question is easy to use:

- What "color" or "sound" person are you?
- Would you prefer to read a good book, watch a movie or listen to music?
- What's your earliest memory?
- What's your favorite quote (or saying)?
- If you had a magic wand, what would you choose to change?
- Where in the world would you like to be right now?

Plan to spend about ten to fifteen minutes on this ice breaker. If you have a small group and it finishes quickly, do more than one round with other questions.

> An Ice Breaker is an opening remark, action, or activity that is designed to ease tension or relieve formality.

If you're more daring and it's the right group of people, you might want to try some of the more formal ice breakers listed below. You also might need more time for these as they involve some setup, so allow fifteen to twenty minutes to complete this section. Hopefully, there'll be lots of smiles, some laughter, and some relaxing.

Picture Perfect

Most everyone has at least one photograph in their wallet or purse. Ask each person to take out a photo they have and tell a story that goes along with it. It can be heartwarming, take you down memory lane or simply remind you of a funny experience.

Name Me

Have each person add an adjective to her name that starts with the same letter (such as Sassy Sue, Blue-eyed Barbara, Dependable Debbie). You get the gist. And then have them tell why they chose that adjective.

Pairing and Sharing

Pair off with someone you do not know. Person 1 speaks for one minute on any subject of their choosing. Person 2 listens, smiles and says nothing until Person 1 is done. Then switch roles. After all are done, go around the room and have each person describe to the group what their partner told them. Everyone has fun with this and laughter will ensue when people get things mixed up. You can also choose to make your 1 minute subject to be "All About Me" where each person tells whatever they wish about themselves, which is then related to the group by their partner.

Compare and Contrast

Split into two or three groups of three or four people. Give each group paper and pen. Ask someone in each group to volunteer to write down their group's responses to two questions. (This can be shared by two members, one for each question.)

First, "What do we all have in common?" To get everyone's creative juices started, some suggestions are: Does everyone like chocolate? Has everyone been on a plane? Do we all take baths? Commonalities can be as grandiose or simple as your group desires. Spend a few minutes gathering responses and then each scribe will share their list with the whole group.

Secondly, "How am I different from everyone else in my group?" What makes you unique or special? Where have you been that no one else has visited? Your group may need some extra time to figure this one out, so allow the time, gather up the responses, and once again report to the group.

When done, a few chuckles and probably some interesting themes will have been shared by all.

What's In A Shoe?

Ask everyone to remove their shoes, put one to the side of the room or playing area, and hold onto the other. Assemble the group in a circle, and ask them to toss their shoe into the center.

Once the shoes are in the center, everyone should pick up a shoe that belongs to someone else. One by one each person should describe the owner of the shoe based on what the shoe looks like. They can include size, gender, hobbies, fashion sense, favorite sports etc.

When they finish describing the person, the owner should step forward and introduce herself. The real owner can verify or deny any of the things that were said about her.

True Confessions

Give everyone a piece of paper and a pencil. Have them tear the paper into three pieces. Ask them to write down 3 questions they want to ask the group, each on a separate piece of paper. Questions can range from "What are the names of your siblings and who are you in the birth order?" to "Would you rather wear a long dress, jeans or short shorts on a first date and why?" or "Tell a story about your best birthday memory".

Yes or no questions should include "And why?" with them to generate more interesting responses. Remind your group this should be PG-rated since they may have to answer their own questions. And funny is definitely good.

Put all the questions in the bucket. Pass the bucket around the circle three times, and let each person choose and answer one question on each pass.

Set the Ground Rules (5 minutes)

This is a very important part of your first meeting and will need to be reinforced at subsequent meetings too. Our suggested ground rules are pretty basic, but must be adhered to for the group to remain cohesive. It should take you no more than five minutes to discuss the "Group Success Practices" with the group.

Basic Ground Rules:

1. Treat everyone with respect.
2. There are no right or wrong ideas.
3. Talk one at a time
4. Listen as well as speak.
5. Keep confidentiality.

If you've created a Group Info Card (see Chapter 5 – *How Do I Get Started?*), pass it out to all your guests. Give them a chance to look it over and then go into your more detailed explanation.

These Group Success Practices are meant to be followed at all times but are most important when discussing the main topic of the meeting. It is at this time the group should be a bit more formal, adhering to the following:

Everyone is to be treated with respect

Each guest is coming to a group to learn and grow. Not everyone will have the same views on topics; not everyone will have the same education or financial stability; not everyone will be on the same page. Snickering, annoyed sighing or eye rolling should never be tolerated.

All ideas are welcomed and there are no right or wrong ideas

Everyone should feel free enough to offer up her ideas or suggestions without worrying that she will be criticized or humiliated. An idea is just that, an idea. It is neither good nor bad, right nor wrong, better nor worse. It is just something to be presented and thought about by everyone.

One person talks at a time

The holder of the talking object has the floor and the Facilitator, or if you have a designated Timekeeper, may stop anyone else who interrupts, gently reminding her that she have to wait her turn. Most times the talking object holder should expect to speak for about two to three minutes. Remind your guests that you will nudge them to finish up if they get too long-winded.

Practice listening as well as speaking

Remember, it's not always about you. It is said we were given two ears and one mouth because we should listen twice as much as we speak. When others are speaking, they have something worth listening to. Other people have important and differing thoughts than you, and you may learn something new from actively listening.

Confidentiality is crucial

It is often said, "What happens in Vegas stays in Vegas." Thoughts, feelings and opinions discussed within the confines of a women's group meeting are to be cherished as something all who attended are privy to. Nothing should be repeated to others outside the meeting. It is only the concern of those who are part of your group. Confidentiality leads to trust, which allows even the most reticent participant to open up and participate.

There will come an appropriate time in the growth of your women's group where these principles will be formally agreed to by all with a Women's Group Agreement. See Chapter 11 – *Taking Care of Business* to find out how to conduct your Group Solidarity Meeting and create this agreement.

The First Meeting Featured Topic (45 minutes)

So much to think about! So much that you want for your new group! Where do you begin? Since you've already shared your reasons for starting this group during your introduction, it is only fair to hear what your guests think. After all, you will be moving forward as a group, and it would be best if you were all on the same page.

Enjoy the process and review the ideas with the group when done. By getting input from the whole group, you'll sense themes and general directions the group wants to go in, and that will help you plan future meetings.

Brainstorming

> **Brainstorming:** *(noun) a method of shared problem solving in which all members of a group spontaneously contribute ideas;*
>
> *(verb) trying to think up good ideas, especially as a group.*

Brainstorming is a great technique for generating a large number of creative ideas in a short period of time. Everyone benefits from hearing the last person's idea and it spurs them forward to think of even more creative ideas.

Come prepared with an easel, a large pad and magic markers to capture all the ideas that are generated. Ask for a member of the group to write down the ideas while you are monitoring the group.

There's no passing of the talking object for this exercise. Everyone gets to call out their ideas as they think of them. It may start out slow, but once it gets going you may have to remind people to keep the noise level down! Your guests may get pretty excited and engaged. This is, of course, what you want. Tell your guests even though you hold the vision of the group at this time, you want to hear all about what they want and expect. No one has to be put on the spot, play with ideas and see where you go.

Throw out the following suggestions to stimulate your group's thinking. Let the process take them wherever it goes as long as they stay on topic. As the Visionary, you may have to remind them of the topic to keep them focused.

- What do you want to get out of this group?
- What ideas do you have for the group?
- Why are you here?
- What does the group look like to you?
- What are your expectations of this meeting and your concerns about it?

Put a date on your brainstorming work of art and save it for the future. Bring it out on your one-year or two-year group anniversary. It will be fun to see the group's original thoughts and ideas, and can be used to remind the group members where they started and how far they've come. You'll all be amazed.

Serve Some Munchies (20 minutes)

It's always good to have some snacks for your guests. Your choice of food and drink is up to you and for this meeting it should be easily prepared and accessible. Remember, it's your show, and you need to be available to run the meeting. You don't want to be stuck creating in the kitchen while everyone is waiting. So, keep it simple!

You may decide to have food available all throughout the meeting, but we have found this to be potentially disruptive, especially for the first few meetings. It gets in the way of the continuity of your meeting if people are constantly getting up to refill their coffee or are loudly munching on chips.

For your first meeting, it is suggested to serve snacks after your main topic is finished. This allows people to chat a bit and share their thoughts with each other in small groups. After brainstorming, hopefully they'll have plenty to chat about!

Your choice of munchies should match what you think your guests would like. No matter what you choose, water should be available to all throughout the meeting.

Close the Meeting (10-20 minutes)

The closing of this first meeting is a very important part. It allows your guests to reflect on what happened during the current meeting and sets the stage for your second meeting.

Steps to closing a meeting:

1. Thank everyone for coming.
2. Discuss the plans for the next meeting
3. Ask who will be returning.
4. Invite guests.

Thank everyone for coming and sharing

Make sure they know how happy you are that they have joined you on this journey.

Discuss what the next meeting looks like

Where it will be held is straight forward. It is usually a safe bet to hold the next meeting at your house again or at the same location as the first meeting. Now that everyone has seen your setup, it would be comforting to come back to more of the same.

On the other hand, if someone offers to host the next meeting at a new location and your guests seem okay with that idea, you might take her up on it.

As for when will it be held, you'll have to feel out your group a bit. Choose a time period that makes sense for you – two weeks from today might work or a bit longer. We have found that one month from today is a good interval between the first and second meetings. This will give your attendees some time to mull over their new experience and get excited about the prospect of coming back for more.

> Having the second meeting in the same location offers a comfort to your guests.

Ask your attendees for a consensus as to when the next meeting should be held. Just set up for the second meeting – don't worry about committing to a permanent schedule right now. That decision can be made later.

Will you be coming back?

Ask everyone to decide whether they would like to come back to another meeting. Don't put them on the spot at that moment. Tell them to let you know sometime before the next meeting if they plan to attend so you can account for how many will come and plan accordingly.

Guests are allowed

Ask if anyone wants to bring someone else with them. New guests are welcomed at this time as you haven't solidified the group yet. Mention basic "Who Do I Invite" guidelines (see Chapter 5 – *How Do I Get Started?*) to help them think carefully about whom they might want to add to the group. Again, they may speak to you privately about this if they are uncomfortable discussing it during the group.

Say good-bye. Shake hands, hug or simply smile as each guest leaves.

Cleanup

Give yourself a moment to relax and reflect on the meeting. Identify high points to celebrate and low points to improve upon. Feel free to write down your thoughts and feelings about this first meeting to share later.

Let's Recap: Organize the First Meeting

The first meeting is broken into a few steps. Follow these action steps to prepare for your meeting.

ACTION STEP: INTRODUCTION
Write out your introduction. Perhaps you want to practice it in front of the mirror. You might be a little nervous at your first meeting, so it's okay to have something in front of you to help you along. See the specifics in this chapter for what to include in your introduction.

ACTION STEP: ICE BREAKERS
Decide what ice breaker(s) you want to try. Gather any supplies you may need. Have a back up ice breaker in case your first one goes quickly.

ACTION STEP: GROUND RULES
Write out your ground rules for everyone to see.

ACTION STEP: BRAINSTORMING SUPPLIES
Gather up or purchase any needed supplies for your brainstorming activity – magic markers, easel, pad.

ACTION STEP: FOOD
Plan your menu, and if necessary, shop.

CHAPTER 7

Chapter 8: The Second Meeting

> *The purpose of life is a life of purpose.*
>
> –ROBERT BYRNE

The second meeting will be an exciting time for all those guests who attended your first meeting and have chosen to come back. If they've shown up, they're looking forward to it and want to see what you've got planned for this gathering. They may not have committed to being a part of your women's group *yet*, but you've piqued their interest, and they're on their way.

You, as the Visionary, are most interested in these people. They've come back for another experience. It is up to you to keep their interest by creating that same positive environment yet adding enough new items to keep them engaged.

Most likely there will be some new people who didn't attend the first meeting, so you do have to make sure to include similar activities as the first meeting. But this time, make it shorter. You can explain to the newbies what you did at the first meeting to catch them up and then get on with this meeting's agenda.

The idea is to follow the basic format of the first meeting. Don't make too many changes until the group has time to form a unit. The routine you started will work for this meeting too. Keep your vision and yourself in charge for this meeting and for up to three to six more meetings, if necessary, until the group is ready to take on a life of its own.

You should expect your second meeting will last somewhere around two hours. Of course if everyone is engaged and willing, you can easily let it run an additional half hour.

> It is up to you, the Visionary, to keep their interest by creating that same positive environment established in the first meeting yet adding enough new items to keep them engaged.

It's a good idea to keep the second meeting at same place as the first, unless your group was comfortable enough to try a different location. This should have been decided at the closing of the first meeting.

Here's the outline for the second meeting. Refer to Chapter 7 – *Organize the First Meeting* for a more detailed discussion of the various steps to follow.

Set the Mood

Your goal is to make everyone feel comfortable and relaxed. Remember to create ambiance and a place of comfort.

Introduce Yourself (5 minutes)

Welcome everyone to your meeting and give a brief introduction.

Start out by saying who you are

Give your name and optionally something about your family, job, age, where you live, your dreams, or your ideals.

Share your reasons for starting the group

Remind the women why you are starting this group and what you hope to get out of it, both short term and long. Your thirty second elevator speech would work well here. (Refer to Chapter 1 – *It's About You, The Visionary*).

Briefly discuss the value and importance of women's relationships

We learn from each other, we share easily, support one another and challenge each other's ideas.

Re-introduce the Talking Object

If there are new people at this meeting, introduce the talking object again. Show everyone your selected item and explain how to use the object to take turns talking.

Opening Comments and Ice Breakers (20 minutes)

Personal Introductions (10 minutes)

Personal introductions should be made again at this meeting whether there are additional people attending or not. It's always good to get a second chance to learn something new about each guest. And any new people will get a chance to learn something about each attendee. This will help them to feel comfortable.

Go around the room and allow each guest to introduce herself. If there are new people, you can have each person repeat what was said at the last meeting – one's name, where she's from, something about herself and how she came to attend this meeting. If everyone is a second-timer, they could each say hi, state their name and then get right into the ice breaker.

> Personal introductions should be made again at this meeting whether there are additional people attending or not.

Ice Breaker: So What Do You Think? (10 minutes)

This meeting's ice breaker could be entitled "So, What Do You Think?" Ask everyone what their thoughts were during the intervening time since the first meeting.

- Were they excited at the prospect of joining this group?
- Did they think it might meet their needs?
- Did they think they might get along with the other guests?
- Was it something they could make their own?

Certainly each person has had some afterthoughts, and it is important to see where everyone is. Some people may have thought lots about the group, others may have simply said, "I'll give it one more try." Make sure to keep it light and don't forget to pass the talking object.

Set the Ground Rules (3 minutes)

Remind everyone of the "Group Success Practices" as discussed at the first meeting. Give out a Group Info Card to anyone who didn't attend the last meeting.

The Second Meeting Featured Topic (1 hour)

Setting up a new group and getting it to work takes much planning and thought. So far there have been a lot of rules and discussion about the group itself and what we are looking for. We recommend splitting the second meeting topic into two parts.

Part 1: Focus (15 minutes)

Discuss the focus of the group. Keep your vision in mind and allow for people to suggest supporting ideas. Review the brainstorming ideas from the last meeting. Use that as a basis to stimulate discussion. Take suggestions and thoughts about how everyone sees the group in the future. What direction should the group go in? What should be included in the meetings?

The difference here is that you'll each be speaking one at a time instead of calling out ideas. This allows for everyone to pay attention to each others' ideas at a deeper level and think about one's own feelings too.

> Continuing to think about the group's purpose and goals will help the group to coalesce.

Remember to keep each person's turn short and pass the talking object! Continuing to think about the group's purpose and goals will help the group to coalesce.

Part 2: Lighthearted Yet Thoughtful Featured Topic (45 minutes)

Now we're ready to get into a real topic, one that stimulates your members' creative juices. Everything up until now has been done to support the functioning of the group – the mechanics, the structure, making people comfortable, etc.

A great featured topic is what will keep them coming back for more. So it's very important that you find something that will make everyone sit up and think. It shouldn't be

> The featured topic for a second meeting:
> 1. Identify the focus of the group.
> 2. Discuss a light-hearted topic.

too controversial or political at this time. We don't want to alienate anyone at this early juncture. Instead it should be lighthearted and thought-provoking.

Here are some good suggestions:

- What does it mean to be a woman?
- Your personal recipe for ... health, happiness, success
- What do you do for relaxation? For fun? For excitement?
- What inspires you?
- We know you take care of others. What do you do to take care of yourself?

If you've got a riveting topic, your guests should get into the swing of things without too much trouble. Go around the room passing your talking object and allow a bit more time for each person, maybe up to four minutes each. Some people will use up every second, others will have shorter answers. Remember, not everyone handles speaking out in front of others with the same level of confidence or comfort. Let those who are short but sweet remain that way – for now.

Use your Timekeeper as needed. If there's time, go around the room more than once, perhaps discussing another topic from your list.

Serve Some Munchies (20 minutes)

Easily prepared and accessible snacks should be the fare for this meeting. Remember to keep it simple. Decide whether you want your snacks available all throughout the meeting or just at the end, as munching and sipping may be disruptive while your featured topic is being discussed. Keep in mind what your guests like to eat, and don't forget the water.

Close the Meeting (20 minutes)

A formal closing of your meeting allows your guests to reflect on what happened during the current meeting and sets the stage for the next and all future meetings.

Thank everyone for coming and sharing

Once again, make it clear how happy you are that they have come back.

Discuss what the next meeting looks like

Where and when will it be held? This is the appropriate time to ask your guests how often they'd like to meet. Spend some time discussing this as there may be differing views. Once a month is a safe bet for most groups, although more frequent meetings are appropriate when your members are craving these get-togethers.

This is probably the first important group decision to be made.

Depending on the type of women's group you are creating, the frequency of meetings will vary. For a parenting group or a study group, you might want to meet once a week or once every two weeks. Of course that's quite a large commitment of time for some people, but your members may be looking for an activity they can delve into with relish -- or escape into for peace of mind. And they may want it quite often. We all need some time to ourselves and for our own growth.

We have found that once a month works quite nicely for our group members. It doesn't overly interfere with our family commitments and working schedules, and it's infrequent enough that we all can't wait for the next get-together.

See if your group can agree on a tentative schedule, whether it is weekly, bi-weekly or monthly. Remember, it's not written in stone. If you start out with bi-weekly meetings and it turns out to be too often, the group can decide to change it to once a month. Flexibility and meeting the needs of the women who actually become members will ensure the success of your group.

As for the location, if you have been meeting in your house up until now, you can suggest rotating houses. This will give everyone a chance to be the Hostess and take the pressure off of any one member to provide her space and hospitality for every meeting.

When we established this rule for our women's group, there were some members who were uncomfortable having the meetings in their homes, so we didn't force the issue. Instead we simply left them out of the rotation until they became comfortable enough to Hostess.

Some people may have young children who would be disruptive; others' houses may not have a large enough space to handle a group of eight, ten or twelve women. Some may live in a remote location, which is not convenient for the majority of the group; yet other women are simply not comfortable with having "strangers" in their homes at this point. It may change in the future, and it may not.

If your group is meeting in a restaurant or some other public space which isn't perfect, you should open it up to the group to find out if anyone has a better location to suggest or an alternative spot that might be just right. Many times people have access to a conference room within their work space or at an organization they belong to. They might be connected to a school, church or club that would allow use of a room on their premises.

> Flexibility and meeting the needs of the women who actually become members will ensure the success of your group.

Different places can be tested out and at some point your group will find just the right spot. Be patient, and it will all come together when it's meant to.

Will you be coming back?

Ask. Then remind them to let you know sometime before the next meeting.

Guests are allowed

It is still appropriate for someone to bring a new guest to the next meeting, provided that your group size hasn't exploded beyond what you're willing to handle. Ask your attendees to let you know if there's anyone else they think would like to join us.

Remind them about the basic "Who Do I Invite" guidelines (see Chapter 5 – *How Do I Get Started?*) before they make an offer to someone outside the group. Again, they may speak to you privately about this if they are uncomfortable discussing it during the group meeting.

Say good-bye.

Cleanup

> *So many of our dreams at first seem impossible, then they seem improbable, and then, when we summon the will, they soon become inevitable.*
>
> –CHRISTOPHER REEVE

Once everyone has left, sit down, take a breath and relax! Notice how your Vision is blossoming. Reflect on how your group is coming together. Certainly this is very early in the life cycle of a women's group, but it will start to form a life of its own with your vision and your guidance. Relish the good feelings.

Remember, you are the one who has been brave enough to take this step and to be at the helm until the group's structure is formalized.

Write down your thoughts before you forget them. Capture the feelings as they happen. They will be something you can review later when you plan your next get-together.

Let's Recap: The Second Meeting

The second meeting is much like the first with just a few changes that will optimize your time together.

Setting the mood, making introductions and participating in ice breakers will all be similar to the first meeting, though your ice breaker will be more focused on personal thoughts of the previous meeting.

After that, it's your job to remind all participants of the ground rules you've set up.

When it's time for the featured topic, you'll break it down into two parts, 1) the focus of the group and 2) a lighthearted topic of discussion.

With that complete, your closing ritual and goodbyes take place, after which you reflect upon your meeting as you, the Visionary, clean up.

Chapter 9: Everyone's On Deck

> *Action is the foundational key to all success.*
>
> –PABLO PICASSO

Review this chart to see a summary of the basic responsibilities of both the Visionary, who acts as the initial Group Facilitator, and the Group Members. This will help clarify what to expect from everyone who participates in your woman's group.

Responsibilities of the Visionary

Provide a safe environment. Be supportive and help each member find her space to feel safe within the group. Allow members to open up at their own pace. This helps establish trust within the group. There should be no pressure for individuals to be a certain way.

Listen and help other members build their listening skills.

Clarify and ask questions.

Set limits and enforce limitations where needed depending on the scope of the group.

Lead initial discussions. Stimulate creative and critical thinking.

Create rituals. Use of the talking object, candles, oils, incense, opening or closing meditation.

Provide Structure. Go around the room for news updates, keep everyone on topic, and give each person a chance to speak at each meeting.

Set up group responsibilities. It's up to you to assign the Calendar Keeper, Treasurer, Dining-Out Diva, Hostess, Facilitator/Topic Presenter, Timekeeper, and Event Organizer.

Create a balance between providing space for members to share freely and constructively handle strong emotions.

Facilitate the group's creation of the ground rules or "Group Success Practices" and have the members commit to the group with the "Women's Group Agreement."

Build in celebrations for the group.

Being a member of a women's group can be an incredibly fulfilling experience. When we look to joining such a group, we typically ask ourselves what this group will do for us. Why should I join this group? Will it give me what I need? However, it is also important to ask yourself what you can bring to the group.

Responsibilities of the Group Members

Treat each other with respect.

Be a good listener. Take time to actively listen to the other members.

Participate actively and insure that everyone has a chance to participate.

Follow rituals created by the group.

Never verbally attack anyone even if it is for their own good. No ridicule.

Take a risk and open up – do it at your own pace, but do it. As you become more comfortable, step forward and share who you are with the other members. Allow yourself to be known.

Be non-judgmental.

Allow each person to get comfortable within the group.

Protect each member's "sharing" within the group and don't share their stories with others outside of the group. Respect their personal information.

Work to establish relationships with other group members.

Commit to showing up on time, on a regular and recurring basis.

Eliminate gossiping about other members.

Be open to make positive changes – come prepared to provide solutions as an active member of the group.

Give and receive feedback.

Offer up your personal skills to enhance the group experience; help where needed.

Use the group to discover and develop new skills. Be open to suggestions (if they feel right to you) and make positive changes in your life.

Expect the unexpected.

Celebrate together.

Let's Recap: Everyone's On Deck

As the Visionary:

- What are the three responsibilities that stick out the most to you?
- Why?
- Which one area do you feel needs some work in your own role as the Visionary?

As a group member:

- What are the three responsibilities that stick out the most to you?
- Why?
- Which one area do you feel you need to improve as a member of the group?

CHAPTER 9

Chapter 10: Building Relationships

> *Never refuse any advance of friendship, for if nine out of ten bring you nothing, one alone may repay you.*
>
> –MADAME DE TENCIN

How nice it is when the women we meet in our group actually become real live friends. Sometimes it happens when your members start to hang out with each other beyond the boundaries of your women's group. These relationships change and grow as time goes on. Our circles enlarge, and these new friends become part of our everyday lives, meeting our families and friends and joining us in our celebrations and life passages.

Sometimes the relationships remain centered around the group itself, and that's okay too. We can enjoy the benefits of women's company as part of the group, enrich ourselves by the experiences we have while in the group and do things together that we may not

> There is strength in numbers and strength in the bonds formed by being a part of a group.

be brave enough to try on our own. There is strength in numbers and strength in the bonds formed by being a part of a group.

Some people come into one's life for a season and your women's group can be a part of your life for a season or many, many seasons.

A Member in Need

Sometimes it's appropriate to let someone speak for a long time until she is done, no matter how long it takes. This would be when a very sensitive issue has arisen for her personally and would fall outside of the normal "pass the talking object" routine during formal topic discussions.

The group should remember that as long as she holds the talking object, she is permitted to continue her story or her experience. Even if she pauses to think of the right words, to tear up or to collect herself, she still retains the right to continue to speak.

> Sometimes it's appropriate to let someone speak for a long time until she is done, no matter how long it takes.

When an important issue arises for one of our members, we set aside the time to join with her, to listen to her, be present with her, and to offer her support when asked for and when needed. We don't usually encourage advice giving, but this may be a time when that rule is relaxed. We like to give this person a chance to have as much time as she needs, within reason. She holds the talking object until relinquished.

We Need to Talk

There are times that an important issue or life passage is center stage for one of your group members. She may request that this issue be part of your meeting's agenda. It's not that she needs to hold the talking object and let down her hair as much as she wants to present her dilemma and gather input from the group and suggestions on how to handle a situation that has arisen. In this circumstance, the group's normal routine may take a back seat to the needs of the moment.

This might happen if one has an elderly parent who unexpectedly takes a turn for the worse. Gathering ideas from caring women about what to do or how to proceed is priceless. Some may have already been through a similar trying time and may have connections to places where you can find guidance or get help. Your group is there to offer support and to mobilize when needed.

> The need to balance is important and the need to have agreement among the group members on how to handle these situations is paramount.

Even a happy life passage or occasion may sidetrack the group in a positive way. The birth of a baby or of a grandchild, a child going off to college, a new job, a new relationship, or a cherished vacation experience are all reasons to want to share with your group. In these cases, you can lengthen the Time to Catch Up portion of your meeting, allowing your member to bring her happiness and excitement to the group without overtaking your entire meeting.

Some flexibility is the key here, and your members should collectively decide whether or not these asides are pertinent or appropriate for your group.

Sometimes we have trouble in our group getting down to the topic because there's so much going on in our personal lives that we want to share with our group friends. Some of us visit with each other outside of the group and others don't have the time or the inclination. So when we get together, those of us who haven't already had any catch up time want to hear about what's been going on in our friends' lives since the last meeting. Others of us want to stick to the topic. It's caused us some annoyance on both sides at times.

The need to balance is important and the need to have agreement among the group members on how to handle these situations is paramount. Some groups may choose to allow these asides and others may feel it more appropriate to stick to the format and wait until the end of the meeting for extended personal chats.

Help Each Other in Crisis

> *When a friend is in trouble, don't annoy [her] by asking*
> *if there is anything you can do.*
> *Think up something appropriate and do it.*
>
> –EDWARD W. HOWE

Women are natural caretakers and many rise to the occasion when someone is in need. Whether it's an illness, a divorce or painful emotional struggle, a problem with a child or a death in the family, the group can be a wonderful support system already in place.

We all want a group we can count on to be there when we need it. Once your group has become a regular part of your members' lives, it is likely to happen. And when it does, it's wonderful.

Karen's Mom became unexpectedly ill and passed away in eleven days. At the time, it was a whirlwind for me. I was trying to hold it all together during those eleven days with my two grown daughters and figure out how to handle each challenge as it arose.

Unbeknownst to me, my women's group rallied and started pitching in. One by one they showed up at my Mom's house where we were all camped out. They brought food for us, went grocery shopping for me, did research for me, delivered flowers, brought good cheer and shoulders to cry on, and were just there to take care of anything that should arise.

I had never experienced anything like that in my life before. My other friends and family called on the phone to check on me ... but it wasn't the same. I've never forgotten how my women's group was there for me.

Here are come easy suggestions for how to help a member in crisis.

- Organize and be there. Short and sweet. And ask how you can best be helpful.
- Contribute funds and send one or two members to the grocery store to fill up the person's house with healthy food.
- Visit often, one at a time. Knowing people are thinking about you in your time of need keeps us from feeling overwhelmed and alone.
- A quick email or short phone call keeps lines of communication open.
- Offer to fill in with covering after school time and ferrying her kids to activities.
- Tell the person that it's okay to call upon the group for assistance where needed. No time for formality here.
- Know in your heart that one day you will be the one in need, and your group friends will be there for you.

Let's Recap: Building Relationships

There will be times a group member has a need. Perhaps the act of sharing that struggle with the group will ease the burden she's carrying. If this is the case, let her speak.

There will be occasions to set aside your preset plans for the meeting and reach out to someone who needs a shoulder to cry on. Other times a member may need more than the allotted time during the Catch Up portion of your meeting to share a particular joy.

ACTION STEP: In our lives, crises arise. It's during these times we need a support system the most. Besides what's listed above, think of three practical ways you might be able to help a friend in crisis. Use the circumstance shared above as an example. A group member's parent suddenly becomes ill and passes away. What can you do?

Chapter 11: Taking Care of Business

Group Solidarity Meeting

At the beginning, you bring your vision to a group of women over the course of a few meetings. Some women have come back each time. Others have come and gone. Still others have been brought along by your members to experience what's starting to gel here. And that's exciting.

A Turning Point

There comes a point during this process where you have a group of women who seem to want to be continuing participants. They are ready to commit to the group and to acknowledge the importance of this gathering. They are ready to attend on a regular basis and to contribute to its success.

> Each woman is an important part of the group's development and when each member comes together with a desire to contribute and build a group, it is successful.

Now it is time to celebrate your bonding together, the fact that you are about to become a cohesive group and to make an official start to "your women's group."

We suggest you create a written Women's Group Agreement, hand it out and ask everyone to sign it. It is simply a way to get everyone on the same page. A celebratory toast, some special goodies or the like might be appropriate at this time.

Your Women's Group Agreement

There are many benefits to being a member of a women's group. Women form new friendships, nurture each other through daily life and grow by learning from each other. Each woman is an important part of the group's development and when each member comes together with a desire to contribute and build a group, it is successful.

Your Women's Group Agreement simply formalizes your group's intent. It reminds them of the basic ground rules to be followed—your Group Success Practices—and asks them to commit to simply being a good group member.

We have a sample Women's Group Agreement for you here:

Our Women's Group Agreement

Group Success Practices

1. All ideas are welcomed, and there are no right or wrong ideas.

2. Commit to putting the meeting dates on your calendar and coming to them.

3. Confidentiality is crucial.

4. Treat everyone with respect.

5. Ensure everyone has a chance to participate.

6. One person talks at a time.

7. Practice listening as well as speaking.

ACKNOWLEDGEMENT:

I acknowledge that all members are important in the group's development, and today I am committing to follow the above Group Success Practices. To me, the success of this group is important, and I will do my best to follow the practices that help create a strong and successful group.

_____   _____

Member Signature   Date

Keeping the Guidelines in Mind

Remember, any time a new member joins your group she should sign your Women's Group Agreement. A small celebration would be appropriate at that time too.

This agreement serves two purposes. It is both an acknowledgement of one's commitment to the group and a formalized agreement to abide by the ground rules you set up. If at any time in the future a member is not following your customary practices or guidelines, this agreement can be used to remind them of the agreed-to requirements of their continued participation in your women's group.

To Name or Not to Name Your Group

Now this is a good question. When you name your group you're committing to an identity, giving your women's group a brand, and that's good. When you don't name your group, how do you refer to it? Is it really a cohesive unit? Will the group stand up to the test of time without a name? Our answer is a resounding "yes," either way.

Some members may want to give your group a name immediately in order to have a sense of belonging to a club or being a part of something special. We feel it may be premature to rush into it, and we suggest that you hold off for about six months before committing to a name.

At the start, the group is all about your vision, your idea of what to include, and what direction you want to go in. Once the group coalesces into a real unit, the direction may have been changed, the ideas you began with may have morphed into something different. Even though this group belongs to you, the Visionary, initially, as time goes on the group will take on a "group-ness" of its own. If you name it too soon, you may find that you have to change the name later in order to reflect the actual goals that have developed for the group.

Naming your group should take a lot of thought and should be undertaken by the entire membership. If it comes up in conversation and the time is right, put it on the agenda and make it the Featured Topic of the next meeting. You could have another Brainstorming session (see Chapter 7 – *Organize the First Meeting*) in order to generate lots of ideas and suggestions.

If no one has mentioned it and you feel that the group is ready for this step, try having a "business" meeting to discuss whether or not the vision is still working. Take suggestions and review any thoughts the group has about its direction. If you're all in agreement, ask your members if they've considered giving your women's group a name. Some may get very excited at the prospect, and others may have never even thought about it.

Make sure everyone is in agreement about naming the group before setting out on that path. Remember that a group without a fancy or catchy name is still a group with its own identity, a place where women will come to share, learn and grow.

Interestingly enough, our group, which has been going strong since 1997, never thought to name itself. We might have discussed it briefly once or twice, but it never went anywhere. We have always referred to ourselves as the "women's group." All of our friends know about our "women's group" and marvel at its longevity and wonder why they haven't been asked to join.

Our families and children all talk about our "women's group," sometimes with pride and sometimes with a smirk – they remember being banished to the basement or to the mall when the "women's group" was held at their house! Even without a name, our group has been a fantastic success, and from here on in it is to be known as "THE Women's Group". It's just that simple.

Some groups get started small with a vision and over time may mushroom into something really tremendous. The group may start a trend, open up new chapters, come up with a product or an idea they want to market and sell. The possibilities are endless. These groups most likely will give themselves a name readily, and they may want to trademark that name in order to protect it from being usurped by some other organization.

The Do's and Don'ts of Dues

Does your women's group want to collect dues from its members? Is there a need to make everyone pony up a sum of money at each meeting? Will it turn people off or make them not want to come to your women's group? Will we be able to share in the expenses equally if we don't collect dues? These are all good questions and should be a part of the business of running a women's group.

Every women's group has expenses that arise at various times, and there are some choices as to how to share the financial commitments among all the members.

Potential expenses may include the cost of:

• providing food at meetings	• tools or supplies
• transportation	• renting hotel or restaurant space
• holiday gifting	• hiring outside speakers
• birthday celebrations	• group outings
• movies, plays, spa visits …	• group vacations

Dues – Yes

Whenever you attend a networking meeting or a business luncheon, there is always a charge. It is meant to cover the cost of any food that is served, the cost of renting the room it is held in and the cost of tipping where appropriate. Some groups add in a little extra to cover hidden costs too.

We have spoken about three different types of groups in this book: Closed Groups, Open Groups and Drop-In Groups. Each type of group may have a different outlook on dues.

For a **Drop-In Group**, where you're never quite sure who will be attending and the players may be different at each meeting, it seems natural to collect some sort of dues whenever a person attends a function. This allows the coordinators to spend money ahead of time on food and drinks or the cost of hosting an activity without worrying that they're going to have to foot the bill themselves.

> Dues may be collected from these members in order to support the functioning of the group itself.

Open Groups consist of a core group of women who attend most meetings and a larger circle of women who attend some meetings at regular intervals. Dues may be collected from these members in order to support the functioning of the group itself. The question arises as to whether dues should be a monthly charge or whether, as in a Drop-In Group, dues should be collected from a participant only when she attends a meeting.

If all of your members are deeply committed to the Open Group, a regularly scheduled dues payment may be in order so that everyone equally shares in the financial obligations. Your members may be happy to contribute in this way to sustain the operation of the group, and it will tend to ensure their active participation. But some members may balk at this and not want to pay for something they're not sharing in when they don't attend a meeting. They have a point too.

Closed Groups are a tight group of women who attend every meeting, participate in all activities and outings and are always in on the planning. It's the same women all the time. Dues can be collected in a Closed Group on a regular basis very easily as everyone participates equally. If your group is one that has numerous expenses with speakers, outings, celebrations, purchasing supplies or meeting room rental costs, then dues is an easy way to keep on top of these charges.

If your group decides to collect dues, a Treasurer is needed. The job of the Treasurer is to collect and keep track of dues and to collect funds for a specific need. If there's a birthday present to be purchased, money to be collected for a group trip, or a payment to be made to a guest speaker that isn't covered by the regular dues, it's the Treasurer's responsibility to take care of this.

Dues – No

There are many women's groups that do not collect dues. Some may feel that it turns a "pure" women's group into a formalized club or sorority-like group and that may turn off your members. It is perfectly acceptable to not collect dues on a regular basis. Groups that don't collect dues work out other methods to share costs.

Groups that meet by rotating in people's homes already share the burden of Hostessing and the cost of purchasing the food and drink served. Each Hostess chooses how much to spend when she provides snacks or a meal for her meeting.

> *Groups that don't collect dues work out other methods to share costs.*

There are no rules as to what is the right amount here. Your group can set a limit or define the level of food that is to be served or it can leave it up to the individual. If one person chooses to serve more expensive items and another has a more Spartan fare, this should not be a problem. It should be understood within the group that this is not a time for "keeping up with your neighbor" and that not everyone is at the same financial level as everyone else.

Some groups contribute equally to the dining aspect of a group by having a pot luck meal where everyone brings one dish to the meeting. In this way the Hostess never has to lay out a lot of money at one time to feed her groupies. It also means that every member has to bring something to every meeting. Your Hostess has to keep track of what is being provided by each member and possibly should assign a category (appetizer, main dish, side dish, dessert, wine, soft drinks) to each member. After all, even though you may want to have lots of desserts, you may not want to have six different salads and nothing else!

Any simple supplies that are needed for a particular Featured Topic are usually covered by the Hostess or the Topic Presenter. If your group requires more extensive (and expensive) items in order to complete an activity, the cost may be shared by the group. If your group knows ahead of time that it will be spending money on supplies at the next meeting, money can be collected as part of your closing ritual and given to the upcoming Hostess.

Think of a French Cooking women's group or a Painting and Drawing women's group. In the former group, vegetables, meats and pastry shells (oo-la-la!) must be purchased for the next recipe; and in the latter, art papers, pastels, charcoal pencils and erasers are needed to make that next still life.

When groups go together for an outing such as a play, a boat ride or a lecture where advance purchasing of tickets is required, it is the job of the Treasurer in conjunction with the Event Organizer to collect funds ahead of time and make sure the reservation is made and paid for. It is easiest to take care of this at a meeting prior to the actual outing. Of course members can simply send a check to the Treasurer in advance if they didn't have the funds at the meeting. In a closed group, it might be easy for people to pay at the door provided that one of the members is able to lay out the money for them ahead of time and is comfortable doing so.

If your group decides to go to a movie together, bring in a massage therapist to give everyone a fifteen minute mini-massage, have a tarot card reader give personal readings, or visit a museum together, each person can easily pay their own way at the time of the service. There's no need to collect funds ahead of time for these activities and no need to have dues sitting in your group's piggy bank to cover these expenses.

Dining out together as a group can be an issue when each person orders different items on the menu. How do you divvy up the check when the restaurant won't give individual checks to each person? Some diners may have a simple salad while others have a more expensive main dish. Some will have dessert or coffee, others may have wine or a cocktail. It's never exactly even.

Your Dining-Out Diva will be in charge of handling the bill. She will try to make it equitable for everyone without being expected to figure out each person's charges individually. That's not possible for more than two or three women sharing. She would need a calculator, paper, pencils … you get the idea. Make it clear that she'll try to be fair to everyone, and ask everyone not to quibble about pennies.

How Are We Doing?

We recommend that your women's group schedule at least one meeting per year to review itself. Reflect upon all you have achieved and assess where the group stands. Review the progress you've made and the group's strengths and weaknesses.

> Your women's group should review itself once a year to reflect on achievements and to assess the group's progress.

Be aware that some members may become disillusioned with the direction of the group or with some of its members, and by opening up the discussion in the full presence of the group, many of this issues may be brought to light, talked about, and overcome.

Without this important review step, you may run the risk of losing valued members when they feel the group no longer meets their needs.

176

Business Issues

When are Professionals Needed?

Should your group incorporate? What are the rules for non-profit organizations? What do we have to know about financial reporting? Do we need any advisors? These are all relevant questions for some groups. Those that have multiple chapters or that provide volunteer services may have to deal with professionals to get proper advice.

We suggest checking with a lawyer, financial advisor and/or accountant to answer your questions. A detailed discussion about these issues is beyond the scope of this book.

Trademarks

Do we need to trademark our group's name? Could there be any copyright or trademark infringement issues? Although you might name your group in good faith, you should first check that there are no existing trademarks on your chosen name. Using a trademarked name is a potentially bad idea since it opens you up to legal action from the original owner.

In the same vein, you might want to consider obtaining a trademark for the name of your own group. Who knows where it will be a few years down the line? It's best to be prepared for the expansion and growth that might happen. Think positively!

Our Group's Business Vision

As your group progresses, you might find your activities have expanded, and you might want to raise some funds to support your group and its future.

There are a number of ways you can raise funds – whether from members' subscription fees or dues, from sponsors, or from the sale of items at garage sales or bake sales. You might consider creating a group Business Vision, which details how you plan to earn and reinvest funds for the group.

Alternatively, you might find you don't want to consider the financing of your group in such technical terms, and would rather deal with things as they happen. If you do want to create a Business Vision for your group, however, it may be a good idea to consult with your accountant.

Don't be put off by the term "Business Vision." Dealing with your group finances as though it were a business does not mean that you are trying to monetize your group or earn money from the members – there are plenty of not-for-profit businesses out there that exist to serve their members. In fact, a Business Vision might help in some ways to free up your time to focus on the actual running of the group and topics for meetings.

If you feel a bit overwhelmed when considering all this, please don't! Simply talk to an experienced women's group moderator, and she can help you to navigate the maze of establishing your group with a name and a business plan. Check out moderators within the school system, your religious outreach programs, self-help organizations, or link up to the many organizers found on the Internet.

Let's Recap: Taking Care of Business

Your group will need to decide how to handle the business aspects that arise. Below are a few decisions that should be made.

1. Name: What will you call yourself, and should you look into trademarking that name?
2. Dues: Should dues be collected or not? If not, how will you handle the monetary situations that are sure to arise?
3. Do you need a Business Vision? If so, how do you plan to invest money raised by the group?

ACTION STEP: Write it down!

Just like you created your Women's Group Agreement, discuss and document your plan for money. Even if you decide against a formal Business Vision, you can still put your plan for money in ink and distribute it to the group. This will allow any new members to be aware of the monetary practices without having to feel awkward at inquiring about how you deal with money.

CHAPTER 11

Chapter 12: Outside the Group Activities

> *It is not length of life, but depth of life.*
>
> –Ralph Waldo Emerson

There are times when the group will want to do things outside the confines of the regular meeting. These activities can enhance the relationships of the members and add to the depth of the group.

Celebrations

Birthday Celebrations

Make it a regular occurrence to acknowledge and celebrate each member's birthday.

Exchanging of gifts is optional and the group should decide whether this will happen and at what level. Some groups may choose to exchange gifts, others may pool money to purchase one gift from the group to the birthday gal, and other groups simply acknowledge a birthday with a toast and birthday cupcakes at the meeting.

> *In our women's group, we go out for brunch or dinner as a group for each member's birthday. It is up to the birthday gal to choose the place. When we first began our group, we would each bring a present to the birthday gal. After awhile it became too overwhelming to have to buy yet another bottle of perfume, bath or spa accessories or a lovely journal for someone who we truly cared about but wouldn't otherwise buy a gift for. So we agreed to finish out the year, buying gifts for each member and then ended that custom.*
>
> *Now we all give each other funny cards and pay for the birthday gal's meal, and if any two people in the group choose to exchange gifts, it is done privately outside the group birthday get-together.*

Holiday Traditions

Sharing holiday celebrations with your group members can widen your appreciation for each other's customs. Whether you share a special meal, exchange gifts or attend a holiday event, start a group tradition and keep it going. Decide as a group which holidays are to be celebrated and find a way to make them special for everyone involved.

> *Our women's group celebrates the winter Christmas and Hanukkah holidays together, and we have used both of the following gift-giving activities throughout the years.*

Secret Santa or Hanukkah Hush-Hush

Each person in your group picks the name of one member out of a hat and buys a gift for that member. Decide as a group how much people should be spending so that everyone knows the price range. The gift is brought to the holiday meeting with a "To" name on it and no "From" name. In this way these gifts are exchanged anonymously. Everyone gets something, and it's not important who gave it to them. It's as if it is from the group.

That One's Mine!

Another version of exchanging holiday gifts is where everyone brings a wrapped gift of a certain value to the holiday meeting. A maximum of $10 or $15 is usually appropriate. All the gifts are placed in the center of your circle. Each member pulls a number from a hat. This determines the order in which to choose gifts.

The first member selects and opens any gift she wants and that is hers – for now. The next member chooses a gift, opens it and now has to decide if she wants to keep her gift or trade it for the other person's gift. Each member who opens a gift may decide to claim any of the other already opened gifts as hers when it's her turn. Go around the room in this way and see just how many times a favorite item changes hands! It turns out that going last in this game can truly be best. Lots of laughter will ensue.

Another version of That One's Mine! is slightly different. Once again, the gifts are placed in the center of the circle. Each person draws a number to determine the order of gift choosing. The first person opens any gift of her choice. The second person has to decide whether to steal the first person's gift or choose an *unopened* gift. If your gift is chosen, you can steal another person's opened gift or an unopened one. Continue until all gifts are opened.

> The group anniversary is a milestone and a time to cheer your success as a group and reflect on where you've been and where you're going.

Don't Forget the Group's Anniversary!

This is a very important celebration not to be overlooked. It is a milestone each year and a time to cheer your success as a group and reflect on where you've been and where you're going.

Do something special, either within the group or at a special place. Make sure to note this special achievement each year and recognize both the growth of each individual and the growth of the group.

Other Celebrations

What about your child's wedding or bridal shower, a milestone birthday, bar mitzvahs, christenings, baby showers? These celebrations are happy occasions for you but may cause discomfort in regard to your group members. Inevitably the question arises: How can I invite some people from the group and not others? How tacky!

Some people establish relationships outside the group and might like to invite this new friend to a celebration. But how do you avoid causing jealousy or bad feelings among the other members who may feel left out or who were expecting to be invited and weren't?

It's better to discuss this within your group ahead of time so you all know how to handle these situations. Come up with a plan that works for all your members. Even though this discussion may cause unpleasantness initially, once everyone knows the boundaries, the issue will be no more.

A *good rule that works for us: If the group member "knows" the celebrant, they can/should be invited, but if not, they don't belong at the function. By "knows" we mean "has been a part of their lives before or outside of the group." No one gets insulted because we all understand. And how wonderful it is when we all "do" know the celebrant and can celebrate together at the happy occasion!*

And Away We Go

> *Every moment is an experience.*
>
> -JAKE ROBERTS

Your women's group has really grown to be a group of women who not only like to meet and share the group experience, but have now gotten to a place where they all want to spend time with each other outside the boundaries of the group. What a nice place that is. So just do it!

There are lots of outside activities that can be done easily as a group. And it can be fun to share these experiences with your group members. In the right tropical location, you might even schedule a group meeting too.

These activities need some planning ahead of time, which can be accomplished by either the Event Organizer or the person whose idea it is. Remember that these activities are not truly a part of your women's group itself, but are extra-curricular.

Suggestions for getting together outside the group should be discussed at the group meetings so everyone may decide if they want to join in or not. In that way, nothing is done behind anyone's back. These get-togethers are different than just a few members meeting for an informal Friday night "movie date" or a Sunday brunch. Below are some examples of these extra-curriculars.

- See a movie, play or show. Have a bite to eat together before or after.
- Take a guided walking tour or boat ride through your city.
- Check out a local museum, planetarium or art gallery.
- Go away on a joint vacation. Try Disneyworld or Las Vegas with your friends instead of your family. It's a different type of vacation.
- Visit a spa or go on a healing trip to Sedona, AZ.
- Visit a national park, go for a hike, climb a mountain, go camping together.
- Sign up for a one-day or weekend seminar at a college on a subject you all like, or attend a nearby conference together.

Let's Recap: Outside the Group Activities

Celebrate good times with your group.

Birthdays and holidays are even more fun when shared with a group of women who care about you. However, as with any other aspect of group decisions, it's up to the group to decide how each special day is celebrated. To make things fair, be sure it's the same for each member.

Occasionally, celebrations outside the group will arise. In order to determine how to handle invites without offending any member of the group, it's important to discuss these with the group as well. Setting boundaries ahead of time will avoid potential hurt feelings.

Chapter 13: The Challenges

> *Any change, even a change for the better, is always accompanied by drawbacks and discomforts.*
>
> –Arnold Bennett

We'd all like to think that everything will always go according to plan and that everyone will always play by the rules and be accommodating to others in the group. A nice thought, but things do come up.

Having a strategy ahead of time to deal with uncomfortable issues gives you the ability to move through them without causing great upset in your group. Some challenges must be handled with care and others just require a simple rule to be in place so that everyone knows what's expected and can be held to it.

Things That Might Go Wrong

Interrupting the Speaker

When you're going around the room during your opening introductions or Featured Topic section, if you use the talking object to signify who has the floor, the issue of interrupting should be minimized. If someone does jump in and interrupt, it should be the responsibility of the Hostess or Timekeeper to remind the member gently that someone else has the floor. And if your members just can't help themselves, well then maybe your next meeting's Featured Topic should be all about Listening Skills.

> Having a strategy ahead of time to deal with uncomfortable issues gives you the ability to move through them without causing great upset in your group.

Your members may have a hard time bottling up their feelings and thoughts as they rise to the top, but it's an art that can be practiced and perfected so that your meetings are able to run efficiently.

There are certainly portions of every meeting when more than one person can contribute ideas and thoughts without stepping on others. But everyone should be aware of the fact that interrupting the speaker is not giving her the respect she deserves.

Each member should have time to state her opinions or feelings without worrying about being stepped on or drowned out.

Giving Advice

> *It is very difficult to live among people you love*
> *and hold back*
> *from offering them advice.*
>
> –ANNE TYLER

Your women's group meetings are about learning, growth, sharing and moving forward. They are a place where you can speak from the heart and know that your group will be supportive. But giving advice is not something we often recommend. After all, people come to your group with different ideas of right and wrong, different views and different goals.

Even if we are therapists in our own right, for purposes of the group, we are not professionals in that area, and it is not our place to give advice. Advice

> Advice giving
> should be limited to those times
> when a member
> specifically asks for assistance
> on an issue.

giving should be limited to those times when a member specifically asks for assistance on an issue.

Starting or Ending Late

No matter how much you love to be at your women's group meetings, you need to remember all your members have lives they are coming from and have to get back to at some point.

It is up to the Hostess to make sure your meeting starts promptly as expected. If someone hasn't arrived yet, waiting a few minutes is fine, but after that the meeting should begin. It is up to the Timekeeper to move things along during the meeting, and help the Hostess get to the end of the meeting in a timely fashion.

Once the closing ritual has been complete, those who need to leave immediately will be able to and any others who want to stay and chat are free to do so.

Running Out of Time for Your Topic

What if your topic is so exciting your group can't let it go? What if they can't bear to stop just because the Timekeeper says so? Well, won't it be nice that all your members are so positively engrossed.

You can decide as a group to extend the meeting for fifteen minutes or half an hour, thereby allowing some more active participation. But after that, it's probably better to continue the topic at hand in another meeting. If it's that exciting, your members will be quite happy to have Round Two at a future meeting.

I Don't Like the Topic

What if someone in your group is resistant to a topic being presented? What if they refuse to participate because it's not something they are comfortable discussing?

If the topic is controversial and makes someone very uncomfortable, either that person can choose to sit it out and just listen or the group may decide the topic is too hot to handle and move on to an alternate.

If someone doesn't want to participate in an artistic activity, for example, because they feel they cannot draw well, or in karaoke because they cannot carry a tune, they should be encouraged to participate anyway. Make it clear that this is not a contest and level of skill is not important. It's the purpose of the exercise that is important, not how well you are able to execute it.

Chronic Absences or Late Arrival

Two of the important Rules of the Road are to "Be On Time" and "Show Commitment." Part of being committed to your women's group is to make every attempt to arrive on time. It is disruptive when people show up late consistently.

> When people show up late consistently, it shows a lack of respect for the other group members.

It shows a lack of respect for the other group members. And those people who forget to show up or have something unexpected get in the way of attending on a regular basis do not show the same level of commitment to your group as everyone else.

This lack of commitment and lack of respect can create strife within your group and will perpetuate annoyance at the offending member, even if your group members don't want to be angry at her.

If this person has been reminded and warned a few times, you might consider asking her to leave your group. A few reminders and warnings should be enough for her to get the message, and if she still doesn't, then maybe this is not the right time in her life to be a part of this women's group. Maybe she needs time to get herself organized or get herself through a trying time before she can rejoin at a later date. This can be a serious breach of trust and respect and should always be taken seriously.

Side Chatting

This is a tough one. It's so hard to keep a room filled with women from commenting to their neighbors or muttering under their breath (but out loud) in response to something someone said. We do have to remember that we don't want anyone else in the group thinking we are criticizing them.

Keep in mind that all ideas are welcomed equally. There are no right or wrong ideas, and no single idea is better than any other. The Hostess, Topic Presenter, Timekeeper or any member concerned can politely remind everyone to pay attention to the speaker and keep it down in the peanut gallery!

> We aren't even aware when we are speaking about others that we may be gossiping.

Gossiping

Gossiping is the act of talking idly about the personal or private affairs of others. It may include malicious talk or rumors and might be second or third hand, which of course can't possibly be the "correct" version.

Think about it.

When you find out something juicy about one of your coworkers or when you know a special secret no one else knows, isn't it interesting how knowing these things give you an adrenaline rush? And many people feel they just have to share this hot info with their closest friends. However, gossip can be horribly destructive and should be avoided at all costs.

191

Everyday Gossiping

Gossiping has been around for a long time and probably permeates most everyday conversations. We aren't even aware when we are speaking about others that we may be gossiping. Most of the time we believe it's a form of sharing between friends or co-workers. Is it sharing or gossiping?

Everyday gossiping takes many forms:

- Calling a person a name, such as "liar" or "cheater," when they aren't with you to respond.
- Repeating a story a friend told you about another person.
- Telling stories about another person without checking the facts.
- Talking about celebrities as if you know them.
- Sharing a negative story about another person, even if it's truthful.

Why Do People Gossip?

People gossip when they feel powerless or when they need recognition. They may have a need to feel superior or want to be cool, a part of the group. They may gossip as an act of revenge when they are angry at another person. Or they simply want attention.

In our women's group we had an ardent discussion about gossiping, why we do it, and what possible value can come from it. We came up with so many differing reasons and types of gossiping that it became clear there wasn't just one perception of what is truly gossiping. So we invented our own working definition, which shows compassion for others, with the hope that the need for malicious, or even just naughty, gossiping will diminish.

If what you have to say would upset the person you are talking about, then it is gossiping.

Good Gossip

Is there such a thing as positive gossiping – saying only good things about another person? If we understand that we are not perfect, nor are others, then we can enjoy the goodness that resides in each of us, so why not share it? This is non-hurtful gossip. It's also known as edification or lifting the other person up.

Women's Group Gossip

In your women's group, many personal issues or feelings may arise during the course of your sharing. As the women become more attached to the group and more trusting, they will become more open. It is very important to protect the sanctity of anything that is shared within the confines of your women's group.

> It is very important to protect the sanctity of anything that is shared within the confines of your women's group.

Let it be known that gossiping about anything revealed to the group will not be tolerated, whether it's to other members in the group or, even more importantly, to outsiders. This breach of trust within and between members of the group will cause great upheaval and may tear the group apart. We certainly don't want that to happen.

Power Struggles

It is not unusual for there to be power struggles in a group, where more than one person wants to take control of either the group or an activity or a conversation. You can diminish this behavior by setting up a group where members participate at equal levels. There should be shared responsibility for monitoring activities. You will rotate Hostesses, Timekeepers and Topic Presenters. All will participate in brainstorming events, take turns speaking, and will be keepers of the overall objectives of the group.

If you sense that someone will leave the group unless they get their way, you may want to allow them to make that decision. Beware of individuals who frequently pose ultimatums. They may say, "Either we go to my favorite restaurant, or I won't attend the meeting." These are problematic as they will disrupt the flow of the group and set up factions within the group. Instead, have the group brainstorm on acceptable behaviors, keep mentioning that every member is important, everyone's participation is equal and stay close to the objective of the group.

Conflicts

Anytime you bring two or more people together, there will be reactions to others, over which you have no control. How you deal with potential negative interactions will be instrumental in the growth of the group. You are not a therapist, rather a Visionary, and you are willing to work hard to make the group a success. Yet, you will need to face this issue.

> Sometimes personalities simply bump into each other.

Based on your guidelines of conduct, certain behaviors are not acceptable in your women's group. Everyone should be respectful of each other, listen actively and keep unpleasant non-verbal cues to a minimum. But sometimes a discussion gets heated and two or more members get out of hand. Sometimes personalities simply bump into each other.

Intervening by asking all involved to calm down is a good beginning. Maybe it's a good time for a refreshment or bathroom break to allow everyone to settle down before moving on. Annoyances can usually be worked through, but larger issues that arise cannot be swept under the rug. They require attention.

If it has never been discussed before in your group, it is probably a good time to schedule a Featured Topic where you discuss behaviors in the group and how the group wants to handle them. How do we deal with others we may be annoyed with? Or what do we do when they remind us of someone negative in our lives?

What's even more important is if you can get each member's buy-in to acceptable behavior for the group. This way you no longer have to work so hard because members will self-correct. After all, they helped create the structure.

Let the Group Decide

Visitors

Should we allow visitors or guests to attend our meetings? How will this affect the comfort level of our members?

At times, one of your members may have a friend or relative visiting them when a group meeting is scheduled. They may want to bring along this person to the group. After all, if your member loves being a part of your group, why wouldn't she want to show it off to her guest? She'd want her friend to be able to experience what she has found in some small way, and that may be to participate with her in a meeting.

It doesn't seem like this should be a big problem as long as it only happens occasionally. Out of respect for our fellow members, you should discuss this and make sure everyone agrees as to when and how often guests are allowed. This should be a group decision. Having a stranger in the group, even for one meeting, may affect the comfort level of the other members.

Certainly it will change the dynamics your group has established, but that's not always a negative thing. This guest may breathe some new life into a group by not only taking in the activities, but by also giving back and participating.

Scheduling Issues

Some groups meet every 4th Thursday or the 1st and 15th of every month regardless of the day of the week, like clockwork. Other groups meet faithfully every Sunday afternoon. But what happens if a member can't make it at that time?

Other groups take out the calendar and try to find a date where everyone is available in approximately some standard interval (monthly, bi-weekly). Will your group be flexible based on your members' schedules? Do you have a hard schedule with your meeting at a set time even if a regular member cannot attend?

It is up to the group to decide if your meeting date is hard and fast or if you are able to adjust to the needs of your members. If your date is hard scheduled, it's very easy for your members to plan ahead for months at a time and not let many things get in the way, but you may end up with less than your full group if someone can't make it one time.

If you float your date based on the needs of the group members, everyone will have to bring their calendars to each meeting so that the group can find an acceptable date for the next meeting where everyone can attend. The good part is you can almost always accommodate your members and have a full contingent at every meeting. Try it and see which method works best for your group.

Our group meets once a month, but we do have people who have very full schedules. So we try to keep it regular, but we sometimes have to change from a Friday evening to a Thursday, and if that doesn't work, we try for Sunday afternoons. These are usually days that our members can make time for. We prefer to have everyone attend if at all possible.

Sensitive Issues

Whenever you bring a group of people together, sensitive issues will eventually arise for the members. Each member is different in her communication style as well as her likes and dislikes, so one can never be quite sure what will come up as an issue. How does this member approach an issue within the group?

Great question and one that all members will want to know as the individuals interact and form the group. In the beginning you, the Visionary, will be the point person. Yet, you don't want to be the one responsible for handling all the sensitive issues as the group members will look to you to solve every problem that arises.

What happens when one member has a problem with the goings-on in your women's group? Maybe she doesn't like someone, and it's becoming an issue she can't resolve. Possibly a member does not want to have meetings in her home because her kids are unruly or her husband will not allow it, but she's embarrassed to say it in front of the group. What if someone uses language that offends another? What if a member feels like she's misunderstood all the time? Or that the conversation always ends up in an area in which she's not well versed?

Before issues surface, it's probably a good idea to work with the group to discuss some ground rules about how they want to deal with sensitive issues. Decide whether the Visionary should handle all sensitive issues, whether that responsibility should rotate among the members, or whether your group thinks it's up to the individual to handle her own issues with the group.

Some members may feel comfortable enough to bring up their issues in front of the whole group, especially when it concerns the mechanics or the substance of the group. The appropriate time to mention that there's an issue to discuss would be at the start of a meeting. Then your Topic Presenter could end a little early or your Hostess could leave a bit of time during the closing ritual to find out what's up. If need be, it could become part of the next meeting's agenda.

> Before issues surface, it's probably a good idea to work with the group to discuss some ground rules about how they want to deal with sensitive issues.

Others may not know how to broach a sensitive topic in the group setting. As the Visionary and the originator of the group, it may be appropriate for this person to speak to you privately about her issue. In this way, you would be able to advise her as to how she might try to solve the problem. With her permission, you may be able to bring up the issue at the next meeting on her behalf. It might even be appropriate to make it anonymous. It may not be important who had the issue, just that an issue exists and should be flushed out.

Handle a Problem Member with Care

The foundation of any group is respect for each of its members so it's important to handle each member and her issues with care and compassion.

Everyone is Different

There is always a delicate line between the group's needs and the needs of the individual. For the group to succeed, its members should be cohesive and handle conflict efficiently and effectively. Individuals are at different levels of sensitivity and need to be handled with care.

Some people are very public and engage with others out in the open, whereas there are members who are more private and would be uncomfortable with any open conflict. The group should discuss ahead of time how they want to process issues that surface with individuals in the group so everyone knows what to expect ahead of time.

Are All Issues Group Issues?

We know that everyone is different and what annoys one person may not annoy another, so not all issues are necessarily handled as a group. Rather, individual members may need to resolve their own issues. For example, if one person doesn't like another person, is it the group's responsibility to handle that issue? Not always. It does become a group issue if their annoyances with each other flow into the group meeting on a regular basis. Otherwise, it's an individual skill that all people need to learn.

A great topic for your group may be "How to Deal With People You Don't Like." Without formalizing the individual's issue as a discussion for the group, if you have it as a Featured Topic, members can share the different ways they handle this problem in their lives. It's a good opportunity for members to learn how to deal with people who annoy them or how to work around them.

How to Deal With Problems in Groups

It would be great if everyone came packaged with complimentary communication styles and personal needs, but that doesn't happen within a group of individuals. People bring their personal styles and issues with them wherever they go and issues could surface within your group and make waves where you don't really want them.

Aggressive Verbal Behavior Toward Others

Some people express themselves when they are frustrated with digs or negative comments towards others. If it happens just once, then you don't need to address it as we all have bad days. Yet, if the behavior is frequent, then it needs to be addressed and preferably with a one-to-one conversation.

Depression

If a member is eliciting depressed behavior, this could be a big issue in your group. One wants to be sensitive, but chronic depression will bring the group down and leave others frustrated and helpless. Unless your group's focus is to handle depression, this member is not a good addition to your group. Your group is not a personal counseling group, and you cannot let her depression become the focus of the group.

If the member is temporarily depressed or has something overwhelming happening on a short term basis, then keep your structure in place where everyone takes a turn to speak and this will be helpful to move the depressed person forward. One can always suggest getting outside help as an alternate solution.

Talkers Drown Out Quiet Ones and Quiet Ones Don't Speak

This is an issue that surfaces in every group. By structuring a time limit for each individual, everyone will have a turn to share. The 'too-much-detail' talkers will have to learn how to fit their comments into the allotted time, and the 'I'm-too-shy-to-speak' members will have to break out of their shells and make an attempt to communicate their thoughts and desires.

The passing of a talking object will certainly help both problematic members come to grips with participating in a fair and meaningful fashion.

Narcissism

A narcissistic individual, one who is focused entirely on herself, feels superior to others, and believes she knows it all, is not the member you want in your group. By definition, this is a group process and should not be centered around any one individual. One of our ground rules is empathizing with the other group members and their issues as well as your own.

This personality doesn't show up in all groups, but when it does, gently suggest that advice is not something given freely, but rather is only appropriate when members ask for help. If the group cannot control this individual's behavior, it may be necessary to ask them to leave.

Neediness

An individual who always has a problem or is always in crisis mode may be too needy for your women's group. Again, the use of time structure will probably help this individual participate fairly with others in the group.

It's important not to respond to chronic crises with an individual. Sometimes this neediness is centered on a death or medical illness and the group should be there to support the individual. Yet, the meeting should not be dominated by this person's issues, rather schedule in time after the meeting to be a support for the member. Of course, members are free to follow up outside of the group to help her through the current crisis.

Non-Compliance

When members don't pay attention to the rules on a regular basis or think that a rule doesn't hold true for them, it can be annoying to the rest of the group. Some individuals just don't like to follow rules while others want to participate properly yet may be uncomfortable because they don't know how. Reminders by the Hostess or Topic Presenter will help to keep everyone focused.

> *In our women's group, some members have always had a difficult time generating a topic for the meeting. It causes them great anxiety. But we don't let them off the hook! It is still their responsibility. And it seems to have become a bit easier as time goes on.*

It's important to address this behavior early on. Trust is built when all members are equal and expectations are equal. And this is good for your group.

Over Sensitivity

Some people are exceptionally sensitive to other members' words and actions and may tend to internalize these behaviors. They may become easily upset or insulted. Over-sensitive people believe it's all about them and react strongly to others' comments and behaviors. It is important to remind them (and the other group members) that anything being said in the group is to be helpful and to advance one's learning – nothing is said to be critical or to be directed against any one person.

It can be a great topic to have within the group meeting – "How to Get Beyond Assumption and Check In With Others." A discussion such as this can help reduce the erroneous perceptions we tend to come up with.

When Someone Leaves the Group

As we all know, nothing in life stays the same forever. However strongly we want to have our group continue the way it's always been, changes happen. People move away; some outgrow the group; some feel they don't want to participate any more for personal reasons. Some may not be able to handle the intimacy or the commitment involved. Others may decide they don't like one or more of the members; some may get frustrated that the group is no longer fulfilling their needs.

> However strongly we want to have our group continue the way it's always been, changes happen.

Whatever the reason, everyone in your group is affected when one person leaves. It upsets the balance and the familiarity of your routine. It is a breach of trust at some level. And your members may be very upset at the thought that one of you is leaving them behind. It is truly a separation and affects everyone differently. There may be feelings of sorrow, anger, disappointment, and at times, relief.

So how does your women's group handle it?

We assume your retiring member has brought the news to a group meeting. After the initial shock, your group needs to embrace the change.

If she is leaving because she is somehow dissatisfied with the group or has had a rough time being a member, it may be appropriate to simply acknowledge that she is leaving. Allow it to happen and discuss the remaining group members' feelings in a subsequent meeting.

If, instead, a beloved member is moving on, the group may choose to share in the moment. Acknowledge that the person is leaving. Acknowledge your feelings and your sadness. Schedule a good-bye get-together, whether it is the next meeting or an outside activity like a luncheon.

Our group has always taken up a collection from the remaining members and has purchased one group gift for the person who's moving on. As food is always celebratory for us, we typically go out for brunch or dinner, share a toast, give our gift, take some photographs, cry a bit and wish our departing member plenty of luck and happiness.

Each of your members will have to grieve the loss in their own way privately. And probably your group will want to discuss it too after your member has moved on. Part of the healing process is getting out all the feelings, being present with the changes and learning how to move on.

Another issue that arises at this time is whether or not you want to replace this person. If your group has been functioning with a set number of people all along, you will now be one short. Give yourselves some time to be without the retiring member and then discuss whether you want to replace her or stay with the group at its new size.

Adding New Members

Should We or Shouldn't We?

Once your women's group has become a unit with a definite contingent of six or eight women or whatever size you're comfortable with, new members are generally not entertained on a regular basis unless someone leaves the group.

It may happen that one of your members will know someone they think would be an asset to the group, someone they'd like to invite. She should feel free to mention this at a group meeting, and all of you can discuss the possibility. It may be considered a good idea by all or it may be viewed as an unwanted interruption. This should be a group decision.

The suggesting member does take a risk by asking the group to add someone new, and she must be comfortable with the fact that the group may not want to go forward with this new member. Also, there's a chance that the group may meet this person and disagree on whether she is "good group material." It's not personal, it just may not be the right fit for others.

Potential new members can be invited to come to a meeting to see both if they'd like to join and if the group feels it would be a good fit. If all goes well and the group agrees, she may be invited back for another meeting. After that, the group should come to a consensus on whether they think she'd be a good addition or not. And of course, she's thinking the same thing – whether she'd like to join or not.

If needed, have a meeting without her to discuss the possibility of her joining. Email is a great thing these days. If it's obvious to you that she seems to fit in, your members can email each other and come to a consensus. If she's right for the group, invite her and welcome her in.

If, by chance, the group decides she might not fit, it should be up to the Visionary or the suggesting member to notify her. You may find that these things work themselves out. If it's not a good fit, more than likely, she will know it too.

If It's a Go

How do you add someone new into an already established group that has its own rhythm and rituals?

> Remember, your new member doesn't know all the "secrets" everyone else already knows.

Above all, try to make her feel comfortable. Make sure to include her in your conversations and try to get to know her in a relaxed way. Don't expect her to be open about her personal issues at the beginning. She has to get a feel for how the group works before she'll trust enough to let the members in on her innermost thoughts. Remember how you felt at the beginning.

Tell her the Rules of the Road (see Chapter 5 – *How Do I Get Started?*). Give her the Group Info Card so she can be comfortable with how the group works and what your expectations are.

Remember she doesn't know all the "secrets" everyone else in the group already knows. She doesn't know how many children you each have or what your job is. She doesn't know all the old stories and the gory details of your lives. So it's important for the existing members to share their individual stories with the new member on a continual basis. Be aware for at least six meetings that this person is new and make sure she is included in the conversation.

The Visionary or any other member might even phone the person and ask how she is feeling about the group. The person who brought her into the group should look out for her and ultimately be responsible for making sure she is included and feels comfortable in the group.

Your newest member doesn't yet know all the basics and it will take some time for her to get integrated into the group. If you've chosen wisely, before long, she'll become a regular.

Let's Recap: The Challenges

No matter how hard you try to avoid them, conflicts will arise in your group. The question is: how will you handle them?

ACTION STEP: Choose one of the following possible conflicts. Write out a script detailing what you might say if you had to deal with one of these issues during a group meeting. Write it from the point of view of the person who has a problem. Then rewrite the same conflict from the point of view of another group member listening in.

- Interrupting
- Starting or ending late
- A member doesn't like the proposed topic
- Chronic absence, which leads you to have to ask the member to leave the group
- Side chatting
- Gossiping
- Talkers who monopolize the conversation
- Narcissism
- Neediness
- Oversensitivity

No matter what the issue, discussing it openly with the group will solve most of the problems.

Chapter 14: Endings

> *If we don't change, we don't grow.*
> *If we don't grow, we aren't really living.*
>
> –GAIL SHEEHY

There are women's groups that go on forever where the only thing that changes is the players involved. Think of a networking group of young female professionals or a school's PTA moms.

There are groups where the players stay mostly the same for very long periods of time and share their longevity with the group.

Our Women's Group is one such group – some of the players have changed over more than fourteen years, but most of the original members are there, and the group itself is still intact.

Then there are other women's groups with specific attainable goals. These tend to have a distinct beginning and end. An example of one such group would be a volunteer or fundraising group.

All Good Things Must Come to an End

If your women's group has successfully accomplished what it set out to do and there is no need to continue, it is time to adjourn or end the group.

Not all groups adjourn. Many successful women's groups pride themselves on continuing for many seasons or many years. How wonderful when your group can continue adding new goals and new achievements over time.

Closing Ritual

It's a good idea to plan an ending ritual at this stage that would allow you to celebrate and honor the group's accomplishments and bring closure to the shared experience. This could be accomplished by simply reflecting on the experience in an informal manner or by participating in a more formalized closure exercise.

Once completed, it may be appropriate for everyone to exchange their contact information, hug, shed some tears, tarry for a bit longer and finally heave a big sigh and say good-bye.

Closure Exercises

Some suggested exercises are listed here. They should be reflective in nature and respectful of the fact that people may be emotional. They should encourage participants to acknowledge the impact other group members have had on them, offer bonding and closure as the group reflects on its shared experience.

Closure Circle

Have each woman share with the group the one most important learning point for her and how she is going to integrate this into her daily life and work.

I Take

Make sure your women are sitting in a circle, as always. Each person in the circle will tell each individual what one thing she will take from that person and bring with her into the future. Continue on around the circle until she finishes. Then someone else in the circle starts. It can be things as simple as "I will take your laugh," or comments such as "I will take your honest and open feedback about how I don't work hard enough."

NOTE: As facilitator, you should come prepared with your own statements for each participant if nobody else volunteers to start.

Bounce Back

Ahead of time, on a piece of paper for each member, create a template of a ball – a large circle divided into three sections. The heading in one section is "One thing I learned in our women's group is…" The next heading is "I was surprised by…" The third heading is "I will always remember…".

Each member completes their own ball using words and/or pictures. Go around the room three times having each person share one of their ideas with the group.

Let's Recap: Endings

Sometimes, a group must come to an end. There are many ways to celebrate that ending. Above were listed a few activities that could be used at the closing of a group.

ACTION STEP: Create another activity appropriate for ending a group.

Chapter 15: The Topic is the Topic

> *Think left and think right and think low and think high.*
> *Oh, the thinks you can think up if only you try!*
>
> –THEODOR GEISEL

Now that you've got your women's group plan of action all ready to go, it's time to concentrate on what you will talk about at each meeting. This is known as the Featured Topic. Having a strong and thought-provoking Featured Topic will make your meeting all the more productive for every member.

We have written a companion book entitled 'A Topic for Everyone: Women's Group Discussion Topics and Activities' with a massive list of possible Featured Topics for you to choose from. We call it our Women's Group List of Topics.

You can easily use this to help get your creative juices going. And when your group runs out of topic ideas, it will provide you with some you never even thought of or entertained.

Selecting a Topic

When selecting a Featured Topic, consider the stated focus or theme of your women's group, the type of members you're appealing to and even the time of year (include holiday-related topics where appropriate).

Our women's group is very general in nature, concentrating on self-growth for each of us. This opens up almost any topic as a possibility, from specific self-help activities and exercises to inviting a Tarot card reader to give us each a twenty minute reading. We have successfully navigated an almost unending supply of interesting and creative topics throughout our years together.

> When selecting a Featured Topic, consider the stated focus or theme of your women's group.

If your group has a more focused theme, your list of topics may not be as broad as ours has been, but it will no doubt delve more deeply into the group's specific areas of interest.

Some women's groups, such as cooking clubs or book clubs, require a fixed topic known ahead of time. In this case, your group will be told that at the next meeting we will be sharing recipes for making healthy snacks, or we will discuss Wuthering Heights so they can prepare for the upcoming agenda.

Topic Phobia

Sharing the decision to choose a topic by rotating the Topic Presenter brings up an issue: not all members are equally comfortable with finding an interesting topic.

"Why can't I come up with a good topic?" is a question some of your group members will ask over and over. Anxiety takes over when it's their turn to select the topic. There's a fear associated with putting oneself out there with a topic one may find interesting or exciting. What if no one else likes the topic I chose? What if it bombs? What if it's boring to everyone else or no one has any feelings on it? There are lots of what-if's.

You will also find that some members are very comfortable coming up with topics. They have an endless supply of creative ideas and fabulous topics at hand with hardly any thought at all. They seemingly pull from their daily lives, their activities, their dreams and their thoughts.

Other members simply cringe at the pressure of having to come up with a topic. It's important to encourage everyone to take a stab at it. Remind the apprehensive members that being a part of this women's group means everyone in the room will rise to the occasion and participate in whatever discussion is laid out.

And, show them our Women's Group List of Topics! There should certainly be something there for them to choose. That should ease their anxiety.

> Check out our
> Women's Group
> List of Topics
> for lots of ideas.

We have found some of the topics we groaned about the most ended up to be wonderful experiences, leading our discussions to places we'd never visited before. Stay open and learn.

Topic Themes

For groups that meet often – say once a week – and have a specific focus, it may be a good idea to have one theme for an entire month. It may be easier for your members to come up with overlapping or related topics to be presented in successive meetings.

At the start of a new month, your group can select a topic theme to cover all meetings that will occur during the month. Then your Topic Presenter can choose an appropriate subject falling under that theme for her meeting's topic.

Groups meeting weekly or bi-weekly might want to have a general theme for each month. In December, a cooking club could focus on holiday cookie recipes, Christmas morning breakfast recipes, Chanukah potato pancakes or applesauce recipes. During February, you might work on specifically "romantic" meals. And in summer, it could be all about barbecue!

Using topic themes to cover multiple meetings can be an interesting thing to try out. If it works for your group and allows for delving into specific areas, keep it going. If your group prefers constant variety, let the topic selection be open to the next Topic Presenter's creativity.

Let's Recap: The Topic is the Topic

Selecting a topic for discussion can be a difficult task for some. By thinking about the focus of your group, choosing a topic will become easier.

ACTION STEP: Create a topic theme list of your own. (You are welcome to use ours, but creating at least a few of your own will bond the group.) You can pass this around to the chosen Topic Presenter as part of your closing ritual.

CHAPTER 15

Our Final Thoughts

> *Flaming enthusiasm, backed up by horse sense and persistence, is the quality that most frequently makes for success.*
>
> –DALE CARNEGIE

Now that you've finished learning about how to create a women's group, it's time to step out and put your knowledge into practice.

The women you invite will be blessed with a new circle of friends, with a support group, and with some good old-fashioned girl time. They'll thank you over and over for creating this group and including them.

As you meet together, you'll discover a deeper, more intimate relationship with your fellow women; one full of understanding and growth. Your life will change as you allow yourself to open up to the women you've chosen to start this journey with. And in turn, their lives will be enriched by knowing you and growing along with you.

We're so glad you've chosen to embark on this new adventure. We wish you lots of joy, the perseverance to continue forward sprinkled with just a little bit of luck on top. Most of all we toast to your success.

And don't forget to let us know how you're doing!

About the Authors

Karen Fusco, a mom with 2 grown daughters, owns Creative Solutions, where she designs and writes custom software, and Creative Properties to manage her real estate holdings. She is also a Busy Mom Expert®.

Pat Brill, a mom with a grown son and daughter, owns Prime Bookkeeping, where she provides small businesses with bookkeeping and human resources services and she founded The Women's Group.

Together Pat and Karen own Boomers In Motion, LLC,
the parent company for all their internet ventures.

They have been active members of The Women's Group since 1997.

For more information about women's groups and women's issues, visit our blog at:
http://www.WomensGroupBusyBites.com

You can also follow us at:
http://www.facebook.com/womensgroups
http://www.twitter.com/womens_groups

or email us at:
info@womensgroupbusybites.com

ISBN: 978-0-9833442-4-7

Printed in Great Britain
by Amazon